TRAINING
GUARD DOGS

By

JOHN WATSON MacINNES

LOKI OF HATHERLOW
retrieving over 6 ft. jump at the A.S.P.A.D.S.
Championship Working Trials

EDITOR'S NOTE

Since the publication of Mr. Watson Mac Innes' earlier book entitled *Guard Dogs—Alsatians—Boxers—Bullmastiffs* both the subject and object of training dogs for Obedience, Guard work and Tracking have become far more widely appreciated and, in consequence, there are many men and women who would like to learn the practical way of training their own dog to be an obedient and useful companion. Until recently a dog that came when it was called was considered "obedient" and few dogs except gun dogshad much further education.

With the recent increase in interest in dog training it has become clear that there are few breeds that cannot, if intelligently trained, have their mental powers and companionship value improved in the process. In consequence this volume on training replaces and enlarges on the author's previous work. It is hoped that volumes dealing exclusively with Alsatians, Boxers and, possibly, Bullmastiffs will follow.

S. M. LAMPSON
Editor

CONTENTS

CONTENTS

LIST OF ILLUSTRATIONS

"Loki of Hatherlow" retrieving over 6-ft. jump at the A.S.P.A.D.S. Championship Working Trials *Frontispiece*

CHAPTER ONE

THE OBEDIENT DOG

Necessity for discipline. Legal matters. Biting.
Fighting. Accidents. Sheep and Poultry

THE REASON for training children or dogs is fundamentally similar. It is not, as the thoughtless would suppose, to teach them discipline in order that they may be controlled, and so be less troublesome to their guardians. The true reason is to give them an automatic reaction to certain things or happenings until they reach a stage of development at which they can apply a process of reasoning for themselves, and thus avoid mental or physical discomfort, serious injury or worse. With either the child or dog it is essential that the tuition should be carried out with kindness, incorrect actions being replaced by correct ones, and implanted in their mind so firmly that the correct action becomes their unthinking reaction. Rational methods of teaching generate trust; so, when faith in the teacher is present, the chances of "backsliding" are eliminated or, at the worst, greatly diminished.

For instance, the eating of unwholesome objects, the fear of being left alone, the thoughtless rushing across traffic lines, are only a few of the serious troubles which discipline or, to put it more accurately, automatic obedience through faith in their guardian's prohibitions, saves the child or dog from during their thoughtless period. When they later become more mentally developed, reason will be substituted for blind reaction, in that certain things will be investigated for the possibility that they are neither palatable nor wholesome. There will be development of the ability to judge distances and the conditions under which moving objects will not be harmful; and self-confidence will replace the artificial courage produced by constant companionship.

The pleasures of discipline arise from these measures, which consist in releasing the dog, to a large extent, from instinctive fear, since the curtailment of impulsive actions will produce a corresponding reduction in the number of situations which cause fright or acts of self-preservation, apparent or real, such as a fight between two dogs, one of which mistakenly thought some action of the other was aggression.

When a dog's training has been carried out properly, the act of living with his owner will be one of pleasure without constant upbraiding or punishment. Disobedience will not be a revolt against the capricious will of an owner but something which produces in itself ill effects and disturbs the even routine of the dog's day and will be thus avoided. These ill effects will be, of course, mostly those which touch immediately upon the person of the dog, but there are secondary results of certain actions which the dog will not understand any more than will a thoughtless child or grown-up. Disobedience in a dog may result in some act which causes a sudden swerve, for instance, by an old and not very active person, a cyclist or a motorist, with every possibility of serious injury either to them or to someone else. It is only when the dog has assimilated the simple rules which will preserve his peace of mind, or his life or that of others, that his "owner" really begins to enter into the pleasures of companionship, and out of this will develop the mutual understanding between the dog and his *friend* which is the real joy of such a partnership.

Some dogs are mentally and physically capable of a tremendous capacity for teamwork, provided that they have worked with a really skilled and sympathetic instructor; such dogs go far in obedience tests and field trials. There is no reason why any truly interested person should not acquire the knowledge to provide this training. Other dogs may not be physically capable of the "clever stuff" but their willingness and intelligence need not be wasted as there is still a tremendous field open to them without resorting to parlour tricks. But even those dogs which are apparently "most hopeless' are quite capable of absorbing a surprisingly large degree of tuition in obedience if the trainer will only try to obtain a sympathetic understanding of their character and adopt training methods to suit the individual, which is in all cases the quickest and surest method of training.

In this connection it is well to reiterate the injunction given to members of training classes by the more ex-perienced trainers—that the purpose of the instruction given at these classes is not so much to train the dogs as to give correct training to the person handling the dog. Classes must, of necessity, last only a comparatively short time; therefore the instruction of the dog must largely be outside these periods and it is then that the quality of training may produce either intelligent obedience or obstinacy alternating with unruliness. The latter is really confusion on the dog's part because he cannot understand the actual wishes of his handler. To explain this state of affairs in another way; the dog has no faith in his handler who often does not know what he wants, and when he does actually have a clear idea of what he wants and the best way to do it, is too impatient and too weak, eventually giving up all attempts to obtain obedience from the dog on that occasion; instead of insist-ing kindly and patiently and with understanding that the dog should do a certain act just when he is told to do so.

There are a number of points at which the law touches the dog owner, who, if he is wise, will make himself familiar with the essentials of the legal aspects of dog ownership. Firstly, there is the licence which must be renewed at the beginning of each twelve-month period, starting from the time the puppy reaches the age of six months. These licences are not transferable to another person.

In this respect it is as well to remember that it is the licence-holder who is responsible for his dog, so that during holidays or at other times when the dog is left in the care of another person, legally that person should take out a licence for the period during which the dog is being kept. The law, however, is liable to wink at such temporary transfers of ownership, but should the dog stray or otherwise get into the hands of the police a licence must be produced when claiming his recovery.

An exemption from liability to obtain a license can be claimed by farmers, shepherds, and the blind when their dog is kept for working purposes. Only one dog may be thus kept, licence free, by each person.

A dog is not free to bite any person, even when the offence takes place on the premises of his owner. Should a vagrant be bitten by a dog, and prove peaceable entry of the premises in order to beg food or other necessity, a claim for damages may ensue. Therefore uncontrolled aggression may be just as out of place in one's home as in the street. Only correct and regular training will make the dog a useful and pleasant companion who can be taken outdoors without becoming entangled with people, or knocking them down, or nipping them if they annoy him. Training will make him a courteous but watchful guardian of the house who permits all tradesmen, postmen, and others with lawful errands to approach, but who is ready to warn of illegal entry and attack at the command of his owner. It will therefore be concluded, from consideration of the above remarks, that it is only from the circumstances under which the "first bite" occurs that the decision of a magistrate can be made, as to whether the dog's owner is liable for penalising, whether the dog should be punished or allowed to go free.

While an uncontrolled dog is liable to "have a go" at

Instructing a Boxer in the "Sit" exercise

Learning the "Drop on recall"

people, whether to bite or simply knock them down, he may not have the courage to attack other dogs, but if he does, the field of damages payable opens out before his unlucky, or rather, foolish owner.

Two emotions probably make the owner of a dog take him into traffic without a leash. The first is showing off. The dog keeps nicely to heel or within a reasonable distance; the owner's vanity is therefore fed by the apparent admiration of other road users. The second is carelessness or lack of foresight, and the belief that the dog is obedient and will do what he is told to do. In either case, something unexpected may startle the dog, or even a combination of normal occurences may do so, and the result may be a nasty accident to the dog or a road user. If the dog is hurt or killed, the motorist should stop immediately, in accordance with the law which compels him to do so, and as the dog was loose it should be easy for him to prove that he took reasonable care to prevent the accident. Should there be an accident or damage to the driver, the owner of the dog may be liable for payment of compensation. Only a foolish person will take his dog into traffic without a leash.

The dog owner living in an agricultural or stock-rearing area must face up to added responsibilities, because his dog will be subjected to a number of grave temptations rarely experienced by town dogs. It is the duty of all dog owners in such areas to train their dogs to immediate obedience while they are accompanying them or any other authorised person, and never to permit the uncontrolled freedom of their dog. In other words, no dog should be allowed off the leash if he is unable to resist the desire to chase or to roam, and no dog should be so neglected that he can leave home for periods of time without his absence being noticed. Mongrels in town or country are often encouraged to get out of the way for a while in order that they should not be under foot. This would be fatal in a stock-rearing district,

B

as it is easy for a dog to get into bad habits or company. The idea in keeping a dog is really to secure a companion who will happily endure such restraint which may be imposed upon him through necessity or for his own good, so that there is no point in having a dog unless he can be looked after properly.

A great deal of harm can be caused by quite a small dog chasing ewes in the lambing season, or cows in calf. Any tendency to do this must be stopped firmly and for always.

There should be no need to use drastic measures providing that the dog has been properly brought up from puppyhood. Any lack of vigilance upon the owner's part in respect to the leisure hours of his dog may result in the latter sneaking off and developing bad habits either on his own or in the company of an acquaintance. These little expeditions may begin as a frolic in chasing stock, which cannot be considered as harmless for the reasons given earlier, and may quite easily develop into killing.

Once an older dog has become addicted to interference with poultry or stock it is better that a good home should be found for him in a "safe" district, because it is really impossible to effect a cure while the temptation remains. It is much better to secure a puppy who can be trained from the beginning to ignore poultry and stock, and it is proposed to conclude this chapter with a few notes on the special training which must be given to the puppy so that the presence of stock and poultry become so normal that they are ignored. This training is only part of the obedience training which will be given to the puppy, and if the dog is trained for his working qualities according to his nature and ability, there is no doubt that his mind will be too well developed to fall into idle habits, and this extra training is simply to get him accustomed to certain new conditions.

The puppy must be made thoroughly familiar with the smell and the presence of sheep; he must be put on a lead and walked past and through flocks, and as soon as he can do this quietly, a few yards of light but strong cord should be substituted for the leash, but allowed to trail freely behind him so that when he shows a tendency to go up to the sheep, or to pay too much attention to them, a sharp "no!" of warning can be given, and, if necessary, the handler may step on the trailing end of the cord and so stop him; the sudden jerk back, plus perhaps a light cut with the free end will· make him see reason. When taken in hand at an early age it rarely happens that the dog does not accept the sheep as a normal part of his life, producing only passing attention when seen and not offering any inducement for closer inspection. Even when the stupid creatures scamper away, he will prefer to walk obediently beside his handler rather than bother to chase them. The handler should, however, make sure that the dog is steady under temptation whilst on the leash, before taking him past sheep without it on, otherwise a partly trained dog will be difficult to break from the bad habit of chasing or undue interest once it has been permitted to start.

There will probably be no option but to give the older dog a good thrashing should he start chasing sheep. There is too much at stake to neglect this punishment should it become necessary, because the life of the sheep and even the life of the dog himself may be forfeited if his training is not thorough. There is a correct way, however, to apply this thrashing, but a warning must be given that under no circumstances should the dog in turn be chased when he breaks away after the sheep.

Try and entice the dog away by walking in another direction and calling him. If that is not successful, then follow him calmly, without exciting him, and order him to do something which will enable him to be put on the leash again. The act of catching the dog must be accurately and deliberately carried out, otherwise if he escapes he will think it is a game. When the dog is securely fastened on the leash again and there is no possibility of him wriggling out of his collar he must be taken back to the sheep, as near as possible to where the offence was committed and be thrashed. The culprit must be held firmly to keep him from jumping about, whilst the thrashing is administered with a leather strap or leash or a pliable switch, and be given a considered opinion (at length) on his wrongdoing. The purpose of the thrashing is not to injure the dog, but to associate pain with the sheep; therefore he should be hit only over the shoulders or hindquarters, nowhere else, and he should certainly not be hit with a stick.

Should it be possible to take the dog up to a sheep, catch hold of his muzzle and press it into the sheep, at the same time squeezing the muzzle until it really hurts, so that sheep and pain are really one and the same thing in the dog's mind. There must not be any form of resentment shown to the dog after punishment: once the matter is dealt with it should be wiped off the record and not allowed to come between the dog and handler for some time afterwards. It will be advisable to take the dog back to the sheep as soon as possible after the offence, on long leash of course, in order to find out if he has learned his lesson. With firmness and fairness, it is possible to train the dog, but should he be one of the exceptions, do not thrash him more than once or twice, but find him a good home in another part of the country or better still in a town. Keeping the dog closed up all the time is not the answer, since there is always the chance that he will slip out, and moreover, it is not fair to the dog.

The potential poultry worrier will probably be found easier to deal with. The puppy should be taken through or near the hen run from the earliest age and any tendency to be unduly interested, or to chase, stopped. At first the long check cord may be used, or, better still a catapult. When the puppy gets a sharp sting in the ribs, particularly when he thinks that his handler is not near, he soon becomes wary of fowl of any description. The method of training and punishment for transgression will be somewhat similar for sheep and for poultry, but the personality of the dog must be studied at all times in order that training should be carried out along the proper lines. Where punishment is earned, it should not be inflicted with the vicious intention of hurting the dog to "teach him a lesson", but only to enable him to understand, within his mental capacity, that certain actions are not allowed, and that breaking the taboo results in pain or disgrace. Where the dog has not got the mental capacity to understand that certain actions are wrong, repeated thrashings are cruel and show the mental shortcoming of his owner or handler who is unable to apply simple common-sense. In such cases, when the dog will not behave properly, it is better to find the dog a good home away from similar temptations, where he can lead a normal life. In extreme cases, rather than repeated thrashings and close confinement, the dog should be painlessly put to sleep by a competent vet. Certain instincts are rooted very deeply in dogs, and in many cases a good habit must be substituted for a bad one; if a dog loves chasing, permit him to give outlet to this in a legitimate way, such as, for example, running and jumping over hurdles, or high jumping.

CHAPTER TWO

THE FIRST STEP

Choosing the Puppy for training

CHOOSING a puppy at less than two months of age is not to be recommended. If it is possible to get one somewhat older the novice will have benefited by having skipped the most critical months of the puppy's life.

When setting out to buy a puppy, a pretty good idea of what to look for should be at the back of one's mind. Shows should be visited, the standard of the breed thoroughly studied, and several reputable kennels should be inspected before a final decision is made. Go to reputable breeders, explain your requirements and you will generally get a square deal and good advice. A lot of people, however, find it very hard, if not impossible, to say "no". They will ask one breeder to reserve a pup, go to another kennel, decide upon what they consider a promising pup (usually at a cheaper figure), buy him, and then straight away forget the first breeder, who may often lose a sale while holding a pup for a few days for the decision which never arrives. A telephone message, or card to state simply that it has been decided not to buy, should be easy enough to send, but apparently is not.

At two months, our puppy should be true to type, have a heavy build, good bone, large head, and of course, a swagger. Any pup who doesn't own the ground he stands on is not worth buying. Avoid the shy ones. They waste time and money, and cause a great deal of worry, and in their turn breed youngsters who repeat the cycle. Great stress is laid in these notes upon the quality of bone in the

puppy. Splendid bone at an early age is the foundation upon
which a strong, well-proportioned and beautifully moving
animal is built. A puppy with poor bone is evidently lacking
in constitution, because a sound structure can never be
built upon a weak foundation.

At about six months of age, the specification is enlarged
somewhat, physical features now becoming more recognis-
able and fixed. The teeth should be strong and white and the
formation of the jaw characteristic of the breed. The legs
should be straight, well boned, and show no signs of cow
hocks. Body carriage and gait is important. Pick out the
friendly puppy who thinks himself "cock of the walk", and
whilst he is swaggering around, have a look at his hindquarters, which should be strong and sound. A dog's
ribs must be well sprung, since ribs without spring are the
signs of a potential weakling, probably concealing a
cramped heart and poor lungs.

The time of year during which the pup is born makes a
great difference to his early development. Spring babies and
puppies are the best off; they have all the lovely weather of
spring, summer, and early autumn to grow and play about
in. Good food with dry quarters and fine sunny weather to
lark around in do more good than the most scientific dosing
with cod liver oil, calcium phosphate, or the various vita-
mins which may be necessary for the winter-born puppy
who, of course, can't help arriving when he does. The experienced breeder does not despise a pup for such inoppor-
tune appearance, but the novice should not, if he can resist it,
go puppy hunting during the late summer or winter months.

There are a few simple commonsense things to remember
when examining the puppy. Pick the puppy up—not by the
scruff of the neck please, but with one hand under his chest,
and the other under his rump, and examine his skin. It
should be silky and attached very loosely to the underlying
tissues. If it is not, but feels tight-fitting, the pup is not in

good condition, or is constitutionally unsound. Next, have a look for fleas and lice. The excreta of fleas, the little black particles which are found in clusters on unfortunate pups, may indicate the presence of these parasites. Fleas are usually to be found on the back of the neck, and on the lower back, just at the root of the tail. Lice usually gather on or behind the ears. While parting the hair in search of parasites, look carefully at the skin. Do not buy a puppy with bare patches or eruptions of any sort. These may be eczema, ringworm or mange.

Avoid a dog with a hare-lip, eyes discharging, bad breath, ears with a discharge or bad smell. Discharge and smells are indicative of a diseased condition of some kind. Discharges from the eyes may be due to turned-in eyelids, or the lower eyelid turned out. Discharges from the ears may be canker or a parasite, which may spread throughout a kennel giving endless trouble, deafness and hysteria being only two of the effects which they may produce.

Examination of the puppy's tummy may reveal one or other of the three types of hernia, or faults in the sexual organs should they be present. It is not likely that the excitement of the first purchase will permit a really methodical inspection of the puppy, but there should be one. Usually, however, the reputable breeder will guarantee the puppy sound at the time of purchase, or, better still, a vet should examine him.

The essential virtue in a watch-dog is dependability to give tongue upon intrusion; what he does thereafter is subsidiary, but should be based upon correct training. The nature of this training must be controlled by the requirements of the owner, the mental capacity of the dog and his physical fitness for the work.

The watchdogs of the past were the Mastiff and the Bulldog. To these were added many nondescript animals, generally a mixture of one or other of these breeds with whatever else was at hand. Taken all round, they were nasty brutes; their environment gave them no opportunity to develop natural intelligence, and their temper was generally ruined by being chained up for long periods, so that the only person reasonably safe in their company was the keeper who fed them.

The suitability of a dog who is acquired with the sole object of training him for guarding, or competition in obedience tests or field trials, may only be discovered by someone with considerable experience, since quite a number of factors must be given careful thought. It is not the purpose of this chapter to discuss the psychology of the dog in detail, but there are a number of things discoverable by means of simple commonsense combined with the knowledge that beauty is only skin deep. The standards by which a dog is judged for the show ring are not entirely those by which the dog would be judged when under consideration for suitability for training. The following notes are put forward as a suggestion of certain characteristics to be studied when choosing a dog for training.

Hearing and sight are fortunately responsive to certain simple tests. Both can be dulled by lack of training or physical disability, such as bad health or old age, but proper training can sharpen the sight or finely tune the hearing. Sensitivity to touch should be noted; it can be dulled by familiarity or kindness or increased by brutality and unnecessary punishment. The clue to the rehabilitation of a "difficult" dog often lies in the degree of his sensitivity to touch, which may tell of bad ownership and the necessity to regain his confidence. Until this is restored and a more normal condition returns, it is useless attempting to put the dog to work, as it will be wasting time and will probably ruin the dog.

Fear in the dog is a rather complex emotion manifesting itself in a number of different ways, ranging from natural suspiciousness or nervousness, which usually have some physical basis, to extreme shyness produced by guns or similar sudden noises. When the underlying basis of fear is natural a cure may be brought about by kindness or sensible treatment, but fear caused by gunfire or other means of producing nervous shock is more difficult to treat, or even, as is often the case, completely resistant to cure. Aggressiveness, like fear, may take various forms, such as considering everyone with the exception of certain people, as enemies to be attacked; or again, the dog may still dislike people but will run away instead of performing any act of aggression. The spirit of aggression may also show itself by the dog chasing people and objects, apparently instinctively, without any intention of fighting. Unless care is taken to curb this over-developed protective instinct it will become too embarrassingly sharp. Most dogs are only too ready to protect master, home and property.

There is a considerable difference between the susceptibility to distraction of a scatterbrain and a naturally alert dog. The natural instincts of the latter are such that he is interested in all happenings for a considerable distance around. A dog depends to a great extent upon hearing and smell, and to a lesser degree upon eyesight. Two forms of distraction, social and sexual, can be controlled by the handler, but the object of training will determine the extent to which other forms of distraction should be permitted. On all occasions, kindness will give the dog the necessary confidence in his handler.

To conclude these notes upon the various characteristics which must be found in a dog whom one intends to train for obedience work or trials, it must be emphasized that the essential which binds them all together is willingness. To secure this, the dog must have a desire to please his handler, and be physically capable of doing the work required. The handler must contribute experience and a love for his task, plus ability to transmit his wishes to the dog.

CHAPTER THREE

ELEMENTARY LESSONS

Good manners. Quarters. Recall. To heel off and on leash

ALTHOUGH THE serious training of a puppy should not start until he is over six months old, he can be taught elementary good manners in the home, and later, when old enough to be taken out, be given instruction on good manners in the street.

Commonsense will forestall the commission of many of these little "crimes" by puppies or even by older dogs. Only the most elementary form of anticipation is necessary in the majority of cases. Put the puppy out of doors first thing in the morning and last thing at night, and immediately after his meals, in order to give him an opportunity to relieve himself. When this function is properly fulfilled, praise the pup so that, in the course of time, he may be told to go out of doors for that purpose with the reasonable expectation that the order will be obeyed. Any attempt to relieve himself when indoors should be treated by scolding and the immediate banishment of the puppy to the proper place for such practices, there to complete the act and to have the fact impressed on his mind that there is a definite relation between the desire and where it may be carried out without incurring the wrath of its owner. Show the evidence of guilt, and scold; only in obstinate cases should punishment be given, when a firm, but merciful, spanking should be administered. Then the culprit should be sent outdoors so as to tie up in his mind the act and where it should properly take place.

One should remember that the fault generally lies with the handler's lack of anticipation of the dog's needs. Never allow a puppy the opportunity of acquiring a habit of uncleanliness, since, once started, it is most difficult to eradicate. Patience and firmness will reduce to the minimum the length of time covered by this awkward period in a puppy's life with the consequent annoyance.

A puppy who is to be permitted to live indoors should have one or more comfortable rugs or cushions in different and permanent places allocated to him, so that he can be trained to lie down on any one of these on command, and not allowed to wander around as his fancy dictates, causing constant irritation through getting underfoot.

Further house training will be necessary to overcome the puppy's natural desire to jump up and place his forepaws upon people in greeting. Apart from the fact that most dogs likely to be used for serious training are generally too large to permit this anyway, it embarrasses visitors and, at the same time, there is a certain amount of danger involved, later in life, to bitches in the early stages of pregnancy. That they are not so inclined to practise this at a later stage is true, when there is more likelihood of an abortion or other serious mischance, but it is a practice to be discouraged under all circumstances. Some difficulty may be met in eradicating this natural exuberance, so it is often more satisfactory to train the puppy to perform some action in lieu, say, to sit down to be patted or to have his paw taken in greeting.

There are several good reasons against taking a puppy to the street before he is four or five months old, but when the time arrives to do so, teach him elementary hygiene. The use of the gutter when relieving himself should be firmly impressed upon the pup's mind.

It is assumed that the collar and the restraint of the leash have become accepted evils, so that the puppy's earliest walks will be simple lessons on keeping to heel on the leash, stopping at the kerb before crossing the road, and on the undesirability of wild rushes or swerves to greet another dog or a person.

There are one or two simple little rules of conduct which the puppy should learn when going into the house with dirty paws. Fundamentally, the object is to train him to stand in a suitable place until he has been wiped down before being allowed to enter any room in the house. The details will naturally vary with each household, but there should be no difficulty in establishing a simple routine which will become second nature.

The quarters allocated to your dog will determine the degree to which he will maintain his health and efficiency. A damp or draughty kennel will soon undermine his constitution; such conditions may be produced by the use of galvanised iron or sheet asbestos walls and roofs, cement floors without provision of raised sleeping quarters, and other constructional faults which allow retention of condensation and dampness from the soil, or afford no protection against damp or icy winds. The outdoor guard dog will generally be housed within an outhouse of some description; this may range from the old-fashioned and, unfortunately, by no means obsolete barrel, through more pretentious kennels, to barns or stables. The inhumanity of chaining a watch-dog to a small kennel has by no means stopped; a number of potentially intelligent and amiable companions are even to-day enslaved in this fashion, ruining their tempers and minds, making them ferocious, witless brutes, their only recommendation being that they bark at every intruder.

A roomy and weather-proof wood or brick kennel is the most suitable for the dog who has to be out in all weathers, but if there is a large outhouse available, all the better, because a wood-built kennel can be placed within it, and there the dog can sleep; dry, warm and free from draughts.

There need be no fear that all this luxury will make your guardian reluctant to turn out to meet the unwelcome stranger; indeed the reverse will be the case, since the comfort enjoyed as he rests will permit him to use all his senses more freely—an open door or other aperture will allow him to investigate anything unusual.

When the dog is to be partly confined within an enclosure, such as a yard or large warehouse, it is advisable to train him in general obedience work, with the addition of the more advanced exercise of "Refusal of food from strangers". The time spent in the patient teaching of the simple exercises necessary to make the dog an intelligent companion is well worth while. To tie up a dog with a long length of chain or rope is not only cruel and uncomfortable, but he constantly becomes entangled in the dragging cord and the constant restriction ruins his temper. If there are sound reasons for confining the dog's range of movement, a wire tightly stretched between two firm supports, one of them to be above the entrance of the kennel or whatever shelter is provided, will serve as a guide for a ring to which is attached the leash. This enables the dog to have a considerable range of movement back and forward under the path of the wire, over which the ring attached to the leash, slides freely. The leash is held clear and is prevented from becoming entangled with feet or neck. In the case of a large outhouse, one end of this guiding cable should be arranged to terminate inside it.

The raising of the bench on which the dog sleeps to several inches above the floor is a simple precaution against dampness and draught. The same raising of his bed will also improve the sleep and comfort of the dog who is kept indoors. It is also desirable that the dog should be prepared to stay tied up in a suitable kennel outside or to be closed in, without reducing the neighbours or his owners to nervous prostration with his whining. Find out if there is real cause for the noise; if not, and it persists, be firm but sharp in quietening the dog by command and gesture, then withdraw and play one or two little tricks to inspire belief und confidence in your "omnipotence".

Until a dog is trained to return immediately to the handler when called, however great the attraction elsewhere, further work is a waste of time. Make obedience to the "Recall" a pleasure to the dog by giving him a tit-bit or petting each time he comes up.

Never call up a dog then spank or scold him for tardness or disobedience. Only a well trained dog, well aware of having broken the law, will come up for a thrashing and this method of "training" will produce sullenness if not worse. The pupil will become unreliable and his actions will lack the enthusiastic fire which is such a pleasure to watch when a well trained dog is carrying out a task which he thinks is good fun.

Should the dog be consistently slow in returning, treat him with patience and kindness, and endeavour to discover the reason why the response to the "Recall" is so poor. Although animals do not appear to employ the same reasoning processes as we do, there is, nevertheless, some reason for the dog's fault, so although it may not be actually discovered, it is often possible to give him confidence and to make him feel that his handler knows best after all.

Some puppies prove difficult in the early stages. In such cases, a long check cord should be tied to the puppy's collar; let him run to the end of it, then call him back, immediately pulling him in gently but quickly, giving him either praise or a tit-bit each time, until he gets the idea that it is always well worth his while to obey a summons. Be patient and you will find the pup coming back without being hauled, in a surprisingly short time. A dog is a remarkable mixture of affection and vanity, so it should be the aim of the handler to adjust the training methods to suit the peculiarities of the pupil. Applied psychology will not, however, be all on one side; the average dog is a match for the smartest trainer whose mind must always remain flexible and capable of instant anticipation of the mental processes of his pupil. The rigid application of a set training routine can only result in partial success. The "Recall" exercise is, from necessity, kept in its most simple form at this stage; in competitive work the dog is required to come up to the handler and sit in front of him to show he has completed the command; then he moves to the handler's left side to await further instructions. This advanced stage will be discussed at greater length in a later chapter. It is important, because the "Retrieve" exercise is completed in a similar way.

When correctly trained to remain at heel on lead, the dog should follow his handler with his head as close as possible to the handler's left knee and the leash reasonably slack. When the latter stops, the dog should also stop and immediately sit down. Such is the exercise under test conditions, but normally the dog may find it more comfortable to stand when the handler stops.

Some training difficulties will be experienced in the earlier stages with backward or stubborn dogs, those continually straining ahead, or interrupting the walk to sniff and greet passing dogs or even to bark or to adopt an antagonistic attitude towards them. Each of these faults must be firmly and thoroughly eradicated. Some trainers advocate a sharp jerk of the leash to get the dog back or up to the handler's left knee; but strangling the dog into submission is stupid and a waste of time, when he can be induced to remain at the knee by giving him praise and tit-bits with the hand held at the position where it is required to keep his head. He will soon learn not to swing his body round, with a little help from the handler. Some assistance can be had by keeping the leash in front of the body when dealing with a dog reluctant to follow, or with it behind the body, with the one

A Dobermann Pinscher guarding his absent owner's handbag

A Shetland Sheepdog refusing food from a stranger

always wishing to go ahead. Even with the useful leverage thus obtained there is a colossal waste of muscular power by both handler and pupil. It is far better to encourage the dog to stay at the knee instead of forcing him to do so. The habit of correct behaviour will be formed more quickly by encouragement than by a running battle of jerks, hauling backwards or tugging forward. Some adjustment of the handler's walking pace to suit the dog will help at first, then, as proficiency is acquired, gradually get the dog used to the changing pace of the handler. The control of an over-eager dog is quite simple. It is not necessary to catch up with him and get ahead to lure him on; turn sharply to the right or even right around, and the dog is behind you with all his tugging in vain. Then get him up to the left knee with a tit-bit and praise. Always get the dog behind you so as to have him come up to the knee.

It is useless to decide to train the dog on leash work when the primary object, for the moment, is to get somewhere. Leave the training of the dog until a more suitable occasion, when there will be freedom to use rational methods to correct faults. These early exercises cannot be carried out while engaged upon an errand, but require singleness of purpose, and a definite and regular period set aside daily for their execution.

When the dog shows some proficiency in straightforward walking, he may be taught to sit or stand when the handler stops. He should be helped by pressure of the hand into the positions required. If the dog has been taught to walk at the proper place, he will be able to adapt himself to right or left hand turns, without a great deal of toe treading at the beginning. Here again, give help in the earlier stages by a word or a gentle tug on the leash when it is desired to change direction, enticing the dog up to your knee as necessary or when there is a tendency to fall behind.

The secret of proficiency in walking at heel on leash is
c

practice, and plenty of it. Keep the lessons short and interesting, use inducement to keep the dog up to the knee, and, when turning, a simple signal to draw his attention to the change of direction, and he will eventually get the knack of it. Walking at heel off the leash is only possible after thorough training in leash work. When the dog can walk at heel with a slack leash, he will hardly notice its removal from time to time. Any tendency to lag should be corrected by a sharp "Heel!".

CHAPTER FOUR

FURTHER PROGRESS

*The Sit, Stand, Lie Down. Distance control – Sit.
Down and Recall. Simple retrieving*

UPON THE order to "Sit!" the dog should remain in that position during the whole time that the handler is out of sight. The return of the handler should not be heralded by jumping up or a dash forward. In this exercise, as in all others requiring the puppy to adopt and maintain a particular position, it is necessary to place the dog in the required position, then give the order distinctly and firmly.

Should there be any attempt to disobey, the only correction is a sharply-spoken "no!" Further explanations or reproaches involving the use of several words have a tendency to confuse the dog. Sharp, staccato orders, always using the same words of command and the fewest possible words to describe the action required, are the ideal to be followed in dog training. Make each lesson short and interesting, and the commands short, sharp and kindly.

Place the puppy in the sitting position, with the order "Sit!"; if he attempts to get up, say "no!" firmly, pressing him down again. Walk around or stand back from him, repeating the command until the idea is firmly fixed that he should sit until told to do something else. To "Sit" does not mean to lie down, so care should be taken to discourage any attempts to do so. "Sit" means to sit, and seated the dog should remain even with the handler out of sight and another person bouncing a ball almost under his nose! In the early stages of this lesson it will be advisable for the handler, when he returns to the dog after having been out of his sight, to go round behind and up to the right side of the dog and stand there. The handler should thus be in position, with the dog on his left, before allowing the dog to get up, giving him no inducement to jump up in greeting.

The ability to stand still and await further instructions is invaluable to a trained dog, but the earliest lessons should begin as soon as the puppy is old enough to control some of his nursery eagerness to bury his nose in food. When the dog is intended for the show ring, a good stance, maintained under provocation, goes a long way towards the coveted "cards".

It is just as easy to make a dog stand gracefully as the reverse, even if it is never to enter the show ring. A dog standing with well-balanced grace, is really an alert dog poised for instant action. A dog with a humped back and legs awkwardly placed has no grace, and less balance; force some sort of emergency upon the dog to produce a state of tension, see the back straighten out, and the legs placed so that it may immediately spring forward or meet an onslaught as the occasion may demand. Proper training will induce the dog to assume this well-balanced stance under ordinary circumstances without having to be "shocked" into the position, which is the only occasion when an untrained dog takes it up.

The exercise should be started by teaching the puppy to "Stand!", while one places the feeding dish before him; he should be taught to retain this position until he is told that he may start feeding by being given some simple direction such as "that's yours". Eagerness to feed should be restrained; any attempt to sit down should be gently discouraged by the placing of the hand under the flanks while giving the order. Guidance should also be given to the placing of the legs in order to straighten out the dog's back. The front legs should be placed squarely and firmly planted upon the ground. The hind legs should not be placed far enough back to give a strained, stretched pose; they should be sufficiently behind the body to remove the unbalanced appearance and humped back that faulty leg positioning produces.

To test for balance, place the hand on the dog's back, press gently down, release pressure, and repeat several times. The reaction to perfect balance is the natural spring of the body back into position when the hand pressure is released. A badly stretched stance, or one too cramped, will produce an automatic alteration of the position of the dog's legs to enable him to balance himself under the slight pressure on his back, and to allow his spine more "play". It will, therefore be appreciated that training a show dog to stand properly is to exhibit the dog's own natural grace, and in every "obedience" trained dog the command to "Stand!" should not only restrain him from further activity, but keep him alert for the instant execution of the next order.

The three positions—to Stand, Sit and Lie Down, require firmness and a clear system of orders to the dog that he may not become confused. By firmly and gently placing him in the required position, repeating the command at the same time, his mind should be perfectly clear as to his handler's wishes. Very often a simple up or down gesture with the hand will prove helpful and greatly assist the changing from one position to another.

When the dog is standing, the order to sit or lie down should be given without unnecessary trimmings, help being given until the meaning of the order is perfectly clear. The alteration of the other positions should be given careful attention; the sitting to the prone position, and from this back to the sitting position explained to him. Considerable progress will be made if the handler sees that the dog assumes a comfortable, but quietly alert, attitude when either sitting or lying down; the latter is not intended as a position to assume for a stretch or a good loaf.

There should be no necessity to use the leash on obstinate

dogs in order to force their heads lower and thus make them lie down. This method, which is sometimes advocated, consists of placing a foot on the leash as it rests on the ground, then pulling the other end of the leash until the dog's head is pulled so low as to force him to lie on the ground. A handler using such methods is evidently out of sympathy with his charge, and would be better to stop all training exercises for a while, or go back to some of the earlier ones until confidence is again established. A dog should be capable of lying down on command, and staying so, either in the presence or absence of his handler, and maintaining complete indifference to distraction. Place him by hand in the required position, at the same time giving the order, repeating it until he understands what is required. The order to lie down should hold the dog in that position until another order is given to change it. The remarks on the "Sit" are equally applicable to this position; to "Lie Down" means exactly that, until the pupil is told to sit or stand. The dog should remain down while the handler is out of sight; but help him when returning by going up behind him and taking up a position with him on your left side as explained in the former exercise.

If the handler gives the dog the impression that he is perfectly aware of everything which he does even when apparently out of sight and hearing, the earlier stages of training will be considerably helped. Many little tricks can be resorted to which will strengthen the dog's belief in his handler's omnipotence. To put it another way, just as personal faith or confidence in his own reasoning powers and ability acts as buckler to his master, so does the dog find the belief that his master is always at hand to reassure or guide, sustains him in difficult moments, binding him to perform automatically what may, to him, be artificial actions completely against reason. For instance, to him the orders to sit, or stand may be all right in their way, but every dog knows by instinct that when he hears, sees or smells anything out of the ordinary, that he should either go up and find out what it is, or duck and get to a safe place so that he can investigate without risk. Training will hold the dog to the spot and prevent him running into danger, or otherwise rendering himself useless by being where his handler does not want him to be. Half the battle is won when the dog feels that his handler is near, and ready to help or guide him if he needs it.

Although the dog has now been taught the three fundamental positions, "Stand", "Sit" and "Lie Down", and to hold these positions with the handler moving around him or at various short distances away, it is sometimes considered necessary to complete the teaching of these by commands given from some distance away. Many people consider that distance control borders upon a "parlour trick" but for those who think it necessary and prefer to make this branch of the dog's training complete, the next step after the normal training for each position is to give the orders from a gradually increasing distance.

In teaching the "Recall to handler" exercise, order the dog to "Sit!" with the qualifying instruction "Stay!", then take up a position some fifty feet distant from him. When called, the dog should come up and sit down close to, and facing, the handler. The difficulties met with in this exercise are either the dog's excessive speed or sluggish movement on recall, or his sitting down some distance away. The handler can make the dog come up smartly and closely by the simple expedient of moving quickly back a few feet and encouraging him to come close and sit. In the case of the over-eager, playful dog who insists upon dashing up and dancing round the handler, the latter should stand with his back to some object such as a fence or a wall which will prevent the dog running around him, or recourse may be had to the check cord which should be hauled in the moment the recall command is given. As the handler is always facing the dog, the latter will eventually realise what is required. Upon mastering the first part of this exercise, the dog is then ordered from his sitting position in front of the handler to the sitting position close to the handler's left knee, to await further instructions. In competition work it is usual for the dog to move, when instructed to do so, from his seated position in front of the handler, around his right side and behind him, finally sitting upon the handler's left-hand side. In police training the dog may move directly from the front to left knee.

One of the trickiest exercises to teach a dog is the "Drop on recall", which consists of recalling him, but, when he has covered only part of the distance, stopping him by the command "Down!". Should the attempt be made to carry this exercise through as an advanced stage of the "Recall", there is every chance that the dog will become confused, with the result that the training gone through in teaching the "Recall" will be rendered nugatory, as the dog will get the impression, upon being halted, that he has made a mistake, and the "Recall" will be carried out with hesitation. It is more satisfactory to teach this when the dog is not aware that he is taking part in an exercise, that is, when he is being allowed to run about freely. The command to "Down!" should be given when the dog is not too far off, since the order and gesture of the hand may not be sufficient to drop him, in which case the handler should go up to him, press him down gently with the hand, repeat the order, and praise him once the idea has caught on. The two exercises may then be combined when the dog has learned to drop while running free, but it should be used very sparingly, otherwise, as already explained, the dog gets confused and becomes hesitant when recalled, expecting always to be dropped half-way back.

The purpose for which the dog is being trained will control the method adopted for instruction in retrieving, which is one of the most difficult accomplishments to teach. The average dog, with the exception of the gun-dog breeds, may not be much interested in fetching or carrying. Some dogs take naturally to carrying a basket or paper or some such object for their master, but the ability to fetch an object on command and place it in the trainer's hands, irrespective of the fact that the surroundings may be strange or distasteful, that there is a great deal of distraction, or simply that the dog may or may not feel like retrieving on that particular day, is something which will require patient and intensive training. If the handler can start with the puppy at an early age, making the act of running after a thrown object and bringing it back a game, the training is greatly simplified. Making the exercise a game is the secret of success in this, as in all other training, and the handler with the use of simple tricks and a little understanding will, in a comparatively short time, train the dog to recover thrown articles. The game should be played daily, and the object thrown only two or three times on each occasion, making use, if possible, of a narrow run of some type in order that the puppy has only two places to go—there and back. With too great liberty of movement there will be a tendency for the handler to have to chase and retrieve for himself, but with restricted movement for the puppy, short and pleasant training spells, with some form of reward, preferably praise, for good conduct, there should be no great difficulty in teaching the average dog, this type of simple retrieving.

However, such amateurish retrieving will not do for the dog who will have to carry out the test under competition conditions, nor should ball throwing and other such games form part of his "recreation" when off duty. The retrieving of an object is part of his "job", so irresponsibly throwing a ball about will have a tendency to spoil this part of his work. At this stage, only a few notes on simple retrieving will be given; details of more advanced work will be given later.

The object used for retrieving does not greatly matter, as long as the dog cannot chew it; a wooden dumb-bell, glove, knotted handkerchief, or similar object, will do. The handler should not throw the object away and then ask the dog to fetch it. Tease the dog a little with it, but show him that the object has some value to the handler, then get him to lie down, go away a short distance from him and pretend to hide the object. The handler should go back beside the dog, let him sniff his hand, then send him off to discover and "Fetch!" the object. It will be seen that the essentials of the exercise are that the dog realises that the object to be retrieved has some value to his handler, and the importance of this point is stressed by the handler who must never be seen to throw the object away. The value of the article is lost when thrown to be retrieved or otherwise treated in a careless manner, and the dog will soon come to realise the fact.

The dog must stay where he is told until ordered to "Fetch!" The object is not always placed in full view, although in training, the dog has a pretty good idea where it is. Lastly, there is a definite association of ideas between smelling the trainer's hand, and the scent on the object to be discovered. More advanced training is based on these simple exercises.

CHAPTER FIVE

THE INTERMEDIATE STAGES

Send away. Drop. Bark on command. High jump.
Long jump and scale

IN TEACHING the "Send away" and "Drop", the difficulties encountered are in training the dog to go straight away from the handler, who of course remains stationary, and, when the dog is dropped, to get him to remain down.

It is the usual practice in competitions to get the dog to go away without having a definite object, although the practical application of the "Send away" and "Drop" exercises would be to order the dog up to some definite object or person and drop him at any point between the handler and objective. When the dog has been dropped, he must be trained to remain down until given further instructions; as the dog becomes more experienced, he should receive tests for steadiness in this respect.

There are several ways in which the "Send away" may be taught, but it will be found less confusing to the dog to teach him to go up to a definite object. Some trainers advocate the use of a long cord attached to the dog's collar, and either run round a post or arranged upon a pulley so that when the dog is ordered away towards the post, the trainer pulls the end of the cord, and the dog is hauled up to the post, this being repeated until the dog gets the idea of what is required. Such methods of compulsion ultimately do more harm than good, because no self-respecting dog cares to be hauled along in this manner.

It must be repeated that in training, the best results are always obtained by making each exercise short, and a pleasant game for the pupil. Probably the following method will suit most handlers, who will modify it to suit the dog or the conditions under which he is being trained.

Select some natural prominence such as a tree trunk, mound, or similar object upon which the dog may jump. Get him to do so, then, by standing a few feet away, get him to run up and get on it. Make a game of it, gradually increasing the distance. If necessary, give him a start by pretending to make a race of it. When he can do this, vary the direction from which the object is approached. Additional places should be provided in order to teach direction to the dog. These will consist of prominences similar to the former, but located behind, in front and on each side of the original "muster" position. He is made familiar with each in turn, then gradually taught to go to the one on the "right" or "left" or the others as indicated. The distance between the handler and position should be varied in order to secure flexibility, otherwise the dog will have a tendency to hesitate or become confused if he has been accustomed to being sent only for a fixed distance while being trained.

When proficiency is obtained, and the dog can be sent off and reach the objective without hesitation, introduce very carefully the command to "Drop!". Plenty of interesting practice, but in short sessions, will win success. It should not be beyond the ingenuity of the handler to modify the "Send away" to a definite object, or to any point of the compass, indicated by a pointing arm, with the help of movement to right or left as a further guide. Some dogs find such an indefinite objective difficult to understand, but most will, in time, respond correctly if the handler uses patience and understanding in his methods.

To make the dog bark on command or alarm is another exercise demanding an original approach to the problem of coupling in the dog's mind, the required act with the command. Upon the order "Bark!" (or the word "speak" may be used) the dog barks and continues until told "Quiet!".

The "Bark!" command should be given while the dog is in any position: walking, standing, sitting or lying down; but in the early stages of training do not confuse the dog by making him adopt any particular position, but allow him to take up whatever attitude he prefers until the idea that he must bark when told to do so is firmly planted in his mind. Then there will be no difficulty in making him bark in whatever position is required; otherwise there is the possibility that forcing him with a set stance at the beginning would tend to couple the order with the position, making it difficult for him to understand when he is required to bark in other positions. Probably the ideal method of teaching is to have the help of a dog already trained to bark on command.

The first requirement is to connect the word "Bark!" or "Speak!" with the actual barking, by using every occasion upon which the dog barks of its own accord to urge him to continue by saying "Bark!" and encourage him by praise. It is not advisable to use tit-bits as a reward for proficiency in this and certain other lessons, as will appear later. Starting in this way, the dog may be set off barking by giving the word, with, perhaps, an imitation of barking by the handler. In this way, house dogs are trained to bark when a doorbell rings or there is a knock on the door. The training will be considerably speeded up if the help of another person can be obtained to knock or ring as required. Some dogs can only be started off barking when they are excited. If such is the case with the pupil, it will be best to do so by means of a romp; then take the opportunity to make him connect his barking with the order.

Points to be observed in training are: some dogs find it difficult to bark in any other position except when standing, which is the natural alert position. Others are inclined, for the same reason, to stop walking in order to bark. Don't overdo the lesson when the idea catches on—a little, pleasantly and often is the best method of tuition.

Advanced work in this exercise is to give the dog some signal which should be as imperceptible as possible, when continuous barking is required, the signal being held until the order "Quiet!" is given; otherwise the dog is to give one bark only if there is no signal. The finding of the object or person searched for, should be marked by the dog giving tongue. When the dog is out of sight, he should respond to name, and the order to bark, so that his position may be marked.

The scope of these latter exercises with the dog out of sight of the handler should be broadened to include barking when faced with the discovery of some strange object or person. In this connection the dog should be introduced to an object or dummy or, better still, a human helper, in company with the handler, and told to bark. Then he should be given practice in discovering by himself the object or person (or dummy), and in giving a proper warning to the handler.

When using an assistant or dummy, different positions should be assumed in order that the dog may become familiar, for instance, with the discovery of a body in any position from prone to upright. It is unlikely that he will be struck dumb, but the responce to the unusual may be only a growl, inaudible a comparatively short distance away, which would be quite useless for the practical purpose of these exercises.

The handler should use imagination in the planning of the exercises, bearing clearly in mind the objects for which the training is being carried out, and using the most simple and pleasant means to secure understanding in the dog, who, it must always be remembered, is an individual, and may not always respond to stereotyped methods of approach to his understanding.

Most dogs will enjoy jumping once the art is acquired but they will have to be taught carefully and progressively in order to build up confidence, judgement, and physical ability to perform. A dog who has lost confidence because of his handler's determination to hasten training to produce quick results, or from jumping faulty apparatus which collapses, will find it very difficult or even impossible to readjust himself, with the result that many promising performers gradually decline because of haste or carelessness on the part of the handler in the early stages of training.

There should be absolute clarity in the dog's mind as to his handler's requirements when he is given a command. This can only be obtained by carefully graduated exercises which develop his understanding and gradually build up his judgement to control his speed, timing and physical effort. The special muscles brought into use by the act of jumping are only developed by practice, therefore it is useless to expect the dog to do any serious jumping before his muscles have been tuned up.

A few words of warning will not be out of place at this stage before discussing jumping and scaling. Certain considerations arise when the dog has been taught to jump and scale; an enclosure which was formerly satisfactory may be no longer suitable to contain him; when out walking in the country the dog will only be too pleased to show off by jumping over such obstacles as may be found, many of these are sure to be "blind" in the sense that the other side cannot be seen. The handler should be very cautious when sending a dog over a jump, and would be wise to investigate beforehand, the conditions on the other side. An experienced dog will normally sense any danger which may lie on the other side of a blind jump; therefore, before blaming the dog for refusing what on the surface appears to be a simple jump or scale, have a look and make sure that there is no concealed danger.

The reason for jumping and scaling exercises is to train the dog to clear an obstacle such as a ditch or stream, low hedge or wall by jumping cleanly over it or, in the latter case, by partly jumping and partly scrambling. Therefore, in tracking and retrieving, the dog will only on rare occasions be at a loss how to get over an obstacle either unburdened or carrying some particular object, which in the case of trials will be a wooden dumb-bell.

The most useful accomplishment for the dog is the long jump and the scale; high jumping, generally speaking is more of a circus trick and not much used, it being more practical as well as more natural for the dog to use the scrambling technique which is used on the scale. Under test conditions, the long jump is 6 feet for dogs not exceeding 15 inches at shoulder, and 9 feet for dogs exceeding 15 inches at shoulder. If a dumb-bell is carried its weight should be 10 ounces. The standard obstacle is 4 feet for dogs not exceeding 15 inches, and 6 feet for dogs exceeding 15 inches at the shoulder.

The apparatus required for the high jump and the scale consists of two strong posts about 8 feet high, each with a bar across the bottom and suitable bracing to enable them to stand upright. The adjustable bars which make up the jump consist of planks 1 inch thick, 6 inches wide, and 4 or 5 feet long. These boards slide down a groove cut on the inner face of each of the posts, the first four boards giving a jump of 2 feet, being securely fastened to the posts, thus serving to bind the two posts securely together so that when subjected to the terrific impact and scramble of a heavy dog it will not topple over. When constructed of substantial members, there will be very little vibration under working conditions. A lightly constructed obstacle is unsafe and, should it stay upright, its movement will make a dog distrust using it. The four edges of each board are bevelled so that when the boards are slipped down the groove in the posts and rest one on top of the other, the bevelled corners on the edges form a series of vee grooves which serve as

Teaching the "High jump"

Teaching the "Long jump"

toe holds for a clambering dog. One board should be 3 inches wide, to allow the jump to be raised by 3 inches each time.

The handler should start with a jump suitable to the capacity of his dog. With the larger breeds, the first 2 feet of the apparatus described above, which are a fixture within the posts (except when transporting), will be used; with a smaller dog, either one of the hurdles which will be utilised for the long jump and described later, or a hurdle especially made, should be used. The first obstacle should be very easy, if only for the reason that the handler may have to jump it the first few times himself!

It is sometimes difficult to make the dog understand that he must jump over; the obstacle looks so low that it would appear to him to be most reasonable to walk up to it, place his front feet on it, and spring over. Probably the handler will have to put a longer lead on his dog and take him over with him, meantime giving the command "Over!", then returning over the jump with the word "Back!" Repetition will impress upon the dog the meaning of the commands "Over" or "Over and Back", but ample praise should be given for his efforts, bearing in mind that the exercise should not be allowed to become boring. Some novices in handling may consider such a preliminary jump much too easy for their dogs; in that case, it is suggested that the preliminary exercise be made more difficult by placing a broom handle on the ground and getting the dog to make a clean and distinct jump over it.

The reason for teaching the double command is that under trial conditions, retrieving over the jump or scale forms part of the exercise; therefore the dog must learn to go over, pick up the dumb-bell, and return over the obstacle. Once the dog has mastered the art of clean jumping over the low obstacle, the boards may be gradually increased, by 6 inches at a time in the earlier stages, and then by 3 inches, using the

D

narrow board alternatively with the wider ones, giving 3, 6, 9 and another 12 inches, repeating again by adding the narrow board, removing it and substituting a 6-inch board, adding the 3-inch board again and so on, until 4 or 6 feet is reached, according to the size of the dog.

The scale is taught in a similar manner except that the height of the obstacle is primarily such that the dog cannot clear it without taking a run. He is seated a yard or two away from the obstacle, then with a short run and spring he should be well on his way over the top. When the dog is willing and is physically capable of doing the work, abilities which will have now become apparent from the earlier jumping exercises, the greatest difficulty which will be met with in teaching him to scale is the spring which will be necessary to get him up the scale before the final scramble over the top. The handler will have by now studied thoroughly the mentality of his charge, so will be in a position to judge accurately his capabilities and devise some method of helping him to learn to spring should this be necessary. Sometimes it is helpful to play a little game of having him jump over a walking stick or a staff held in the hand which will impart the idea of the spring, there being no rigidity in such an object, and if he is discouraged from taking a good run at it, he will eventually learn to clear it by springing. Another difficulty will perhaps occur as the dog reaches the top of the scale; there may be some hesitation before going over, and it is important that he should not lose momentum otherwise balance is gone and he will fall back. Encouragement and perhaps a tactful and gentle helping hand in these early stages will work wonders, but never under any circumstances push the dog beyond his capabilities or tolerate conditions which may produce an injury.

The apparatus for the long jump consists of, say, five boards about 6 inches wide by about 5 feet long with a stand or post at each end in order to hold the top edge of the board about 10 inches above the ground and at such an angle that when these hurdles are placed in position to give the standard lengths of 6 or 9 feet the surfaces of the different boards appear to the dog from the low level at which he views them, to be all one plane so that he is not distracted before jumping by seeing a number of landing places between the boards. For safeguarding the dog, should he fall short in his jump, the stands are made to fall back (in the direction of jumping) should he not clear them properly.

Using safe hurdles of this type, the dog is not, of course, sent to jump over them on the way back but must go round to the front again, because the boards fall over in one direction only. There will be a little variation in the height and length of the hurdles as normally they nest into each other for transportation and in such cases the jump will be made up from the lowest hurdle at the beginning to the highest at the back. A coat of white paint will give visibility. Again, as in the earlier jumping lessons, begin by easy jumps, two hurdles about half a yard apart, gradually increasing the distance by the addition of more hurdles until full-length jumping for the size of the dog is reached. In the earlier jumps it will be helpful if a long leash is used, the handler running parallel with the dog as he approaches the hurdles, encouraging him as they are reached and cleared. The dog will eventually learn the pace and length of run necessary, but the earlier attempts should be paced by the handler who should cover the ground with speed and full-blooded enthusiasm in order to give the game zip and to encourage the expenditure of muscular effort so necessary to carry the dog over.

Detailed instructions regarding training for competitive jumping cannot be given within the small compass of this volume because the handler must obtain experience by attending as many trials as possible and thereby acquiring knowledge of technique and timing from the top-ranking exhibitors.

Only by a close study of methods, tactful conversation and reasoning is it possible to succeed in learning how to train a dog, not only in jumping, but the in preparation for other tests.

CHAPTER SIX

ADVANCED WORK

Refusal of food. Guarding free and attached. Scent discrimination. Training Societies

REFUSAL OF food from strangers forms part of guarding work proper, and consists of training the dog to resist all offers of food and drink from anyone but his handler. Start the exercise by "downing" the dog, then place some scraps of a favourite food in front of him. Any attempt to eat these should be met with a gentle slap on the nose, and with the reprimand "don't touch!" When this part of the exercise is understood, the handler may stand some distance away, any attempt to touch the food or drink being sharply rebuked.

The extension of this preliminary training is for the handler to go away out of the dog's sight, having made arrangements to hide where the dog cannot see him, but from where the dog's actions may be clearly seen. Failing such a hiding place where the dog may be kept under surveillance, arrangements can be made with a friend to watch and signal unobtrusively, so that any attempt to touch the food is instantly checked by the handlers' stern order "Don't touch!" Such a command, apparently coming out of the blue, makes the dog think that, even when out of sight, his handler still knows what he is doing. Little tricks such as this secure for the handler an "omnipotence" which is a valuable training aid. Patience and practice will be fruitful in this as in other exercises.

Vary the kind of food or drink given as bait; scatter some around him to increase the temptation, but never, under any circumstances, give the "props" in the exercise or any other food to the dog upon completion of the exercise. Praise him, but no food! If the dog has become accustomed to getting the bait after the exercise, then the habit is formed of temptation—praise—then acceptance upon re-offer. If training is with solid food only, the possibility exists that a drink of any kind will be accepted.

When the dog is steady under temptation from his handler, someone, either a stranger or some person normally having little contact with the dog, should be pressed into service to offer food. A smart slap on the nose should be the reward given to the dog for any attempt to take it or show interest by sniffing. Again there must be patience and practice with frequent changes of people to offer food, so that the dog will get to understand that food or drink must be refused under all circumstances not only from certain people but from anyone unless specifically instructed by his handler that he may eat whatever is set before him.

Under test conditions, several legitimate little artifices may be practised by the judge upon the dog in order to tempt him to accept food. What is more natural for the dog than to catch a tit-bit gently thrown to him! After it has been caught some dogs will guiltily drop it, but the bait has then been accepted. Most dogs, however, once finding the morsel in their mouths, will swallow. With a little knowledge of the psychology of the dog, experience gained from watching other trainers, and observing the methods of enticement adopted by judges in the ring, the list of tricks by which the dog can be caught can be considerably extended, but the handler must remember that the actual "inoculation" of his dog will have to be done by others.

The handler must be on his guard against the possibility of his dog finding and eating appetising food during tracking. A criminal who has studied the conditions under which a crime must be committed (as will happen in the majority of cases) can quite easily arrange to drop poisoned bait behind him. Some handlers nip in the bud any tendency on the part of their dog to have a quick snack in passing, by placing break-back rat traps on the trail. They tie the meat or other bait well down so that it is not easily removable, the trap is well concealed so that the tracker can only see and smell the tempting bait. There is no real damage done when the trap is sprung, but the treatment is very effective.

Under the general term "guarding" may be included the custody of the property of the dog's owner. This appears to be instinctive in some dogs but may require a considerable amount of training to instil into others. Guarding is carried out either with the dog attached by a leash or chain to the object, or by the dog, free from any means of restraint other than training, staying beside the object and withstanding all forms of enticement designed to draw him away from it.

There must be a definite object in training the dog for guarding, because not only does the objective determine the type of training by which proficiency is to be reached, but these exercises approach "man-work" with its dangerous possibilities, and will require an experienced handler and careful training of the dog. Should the objective be simply to have the dog look after a shopping basket, there is the possibility that in inexperienced hands, innocent passers-by may get a severe nip, through unwittingly getting too close to the article being guarded.

Before this exercise can be properly taught, the dog must be proficient in "obedience"—"Heel", on and off the leash, "Recall to handler", the "Long Down", etc. While the handler may begin the training, the main part of it must be performed by strangers or those having otherwise little to do with the dog, the reason being that the handler must never undermine the dog's faith and obedience by provoking him or playing at being an "enemy" one moment and a "friend" the next. Get the dog used to lying down quietly beside the article, instructing him to "Guard it!" When this can be done without the dog playing with the article or touching it, gradually get him used to one or more people walking past within a foot or two, apparently paying no attention either to the dog or to the article.

The next step is for the handler to approach the dog slowly, meantime keeping eyes off the dog, and begin to reach for the article, while urging him to "Bark!" or "Speak!" When the dog obeys the handler withdraws quickly, as if nervous. Repeat, until the idea of barking when any attempt to touch the article is made has been firmly impressed, but never actually touch the article. When the exercise is over, behave naturally, and let the dog know that the work is done for the time being. It is never wise for the handler to carry the exercise further. A stranger must take over from here; the hesitating approach, attempt to touch article and the jump back to safety when the dog barks. The article must never be touched by handler or stranger in this exercise; always *attempt* to touch and pick up only after the exercise is called off. The handler must terminate the exercise whether he or the stranger takes part. The dog must never be allowed to be praised, patted or ordered by the latter.

It will be remembered that in describing the "Retrieve", the dog was made to understand that the article which had to be found was of value to his handler, and before being despatched to find it, the scent of the handler's hand was connected in his mind with the hidden object.

In Scent Discrimination, test conditions may require that the dog pick out this object from a group of others which, of course, should never have been touched by the handler, otherwise they will be contaminated by the scent from his hand and so confuse the dog.

In this exercise the handler may start by carrying out an advanced form of retrieve, letting the dog see him actually placing the object amongst the others, then returning to the dog and letting him sniff the hand before sending to retrieve. Start with one other article in addition to that belonging to the handler, gradually increasing the number until a couple of dozen others are placed around the handler's article, all separated from each other by about one foot. The position of the article belonging to the handler should be constantly changed in relation to the others in order that scent and position should not be connected in the dog's mind. The other objects used in this exercise must never have been touched by the handler, who may, however, for convenience place other person's articles in position with the aid of a pair of tongs.

When practising, it will be advisable to include metal objects such as keys, small tins, etc., to be retrieved, as these are usually included in the official test, because some dogs do not like carrying metal, and there is an added difficulty in that metals do not retain scent so well.

In the early stages, the dog will respond to encouragement, and if the dog has been progressively and sensibly trained, a gentle "no!" is all that will be required for scolding, with the injunction to "Seek!" Be sure that the objects are well handled for some time before the test, in order to have them properly impregnated with the scent.

From an article touched by the handler, the exercise may expand to articles touched by others. The "Retrieve" exercise may be repeated, but this time another person should let the dog smell the article, then go through the pantomime of wiping his feet on the ground or kicking it up a few feet in front of the dog, which is held on leash by the handler, who keeps his attention strictly directed to what is going on. The object is to get the dog interested in the beginning of the trail which the other person makes, and who now goes up to the place where the article is to be hidden, which should not be at a greater distance than about forty feet. Again pantomime helps to impress the dog by catching his interest in the "hiding" of the article, so that every move is followed;

then the other person makes a wide circuit to get behind dog and handler. The dog is taken to where the ground has been disturbed by the kicking, and encouraged to follow the track to where the object was placed.

By the aid of gloves or other duplicate objects having the same scent, the dog may be taught to search for a person placed in a group. A glove is given him to smell; then the dog is encouraged to inspect a group of people, one of whom holds the other glove in a convenient position, but not so that the dog's attention is immediately drawn to it. When found, the dog is taught to bark at the finding.

Training Societies of course, only keep alive through the keenness of their members, and it is this keenness which makes them turn out for training all the year round, and compete at matches, shows, and trials near home and at uncomfortable distances away. It would be difficult to beat the records of Miss Rosemary Coulson, or Robert Lock.

Miss Coulson's dog "Shep" is shown demonstrating certain exercises in Figure 5, and the astonishing career of both Shep and her mistress is briefly as follows:

Rosemary found Shep in 1947, the puppy being then about three months old. After enquiries, the police traced the owners who gave the puppy to her. Rosemary then put her dog into training and in 1951, at the age of sixteen years, she qualified Shep C.D. Ex. at the A.S.P.A.D.S. trials and two years later she qualified her U.D. Ex. I am not aware of anyone having trained a dog and secured qualifications at such an early age as Miss Coulson. To watch her either demonstrating or teaching is a revelation, she understands dogs and they cannot help but respond by doing things for her which they would not apparently do for handlers having more years of experience. Following closely upon Rosemary's record, Robert Lock, at the age of seventeen years, qualified his dog Lulliboi of St. Elyvic, C.D. Ex.

Probably the largest breed club in the British Isles is the

British Alsatian Association, which grew out of a small club formed in 1934 named the Birmingham and District Alsatian Club. With expansion, the title was changed in 1936 to the Midland Alsatian Association, and the present title was adopted in 1946.

The continual expansion of the Association, proves the advantages to be gained from a businesslike administration and the formation of local branches. The work which the branches perform in addition to holding training classes is invaluable: they hold lectures, quizzes, discussions and social meetings, which not only furnish the novice with valuable experience, but promote such a happy fellowship between all members that people who may have had a rather sad experience of the coldness, and infrequent meetings of other breed clubs, are astonished at the friendly helpful attitude of the members.

Every Sunday branches hold obedience and ringcraft training classes under the supervision of a competent instructor. These classes are always well attended by novice and experienced exhibitors and it would be no exaggeration to state that attendance at the various activities of a local branch furnishes the novice with valuable experience in training, ringcraft, breeding, etc., which would otherwise take him years to acquire.

The well-trained dog isn't so much fun if he cannot be shown off to others, so he will be entered as a matter of course at one or other working trials held by the Associated Sheep, Police and Army Dog Society. Details of tests, taken from schedules of championship working trials are given elsewhere by courtesy of the Society, from which may be gathered the nature of the comprehensive tests which the Society holds at frequent intervals, and the standard of training which is required in order to pass each type of test. Local branches of this society usually hold weekly training classes.

Although the Boxer's working qualities have been appreciated on the continent for a number of years, where many are used for military and police duties, the Boxer in Britain has been purely a show dog. As numbers increase, his companionable qualities are being recognised, but this splendid breed is still not being generally used for the purpose for which it was bred.

The London and Home Counties Boxer Club is the first Boxer breed club in Britain to hold training classes for obedience and trials work. At the inception of this club of which I am Hon. Secretary, my wife and I fought to insert and retain in the proposed rules, that one of the aims of the club would be to hold training classes and obedience tests. For some time, the show qualities of the Boxer blinded the average breeder, so we were content to wait. With the entry into the club of enthusiasts like Mr. Fred Cherrett and Capt. Roy Hemsley the almost forgotten little rule about training came to life, as we had hoped. The first training class was held in Clapham, by Mrs. H. Mac Innes, another was started in Barnet, by Capt. Hemsley and Mr. Fred Cherrett. At the Club's first open show a Boxer won high places in the obedience classes in competition with experienced Alsatians, Dobermann Pinschers and Sheepdogs; thus justifying our faith in the trainable qualities of the breed.

In the following chapter particulars are given of the standard of training required for working trials. Even should competition work not be planned for your dog, a thorough understanding of the work which may be expected from a dog under competition conditions is desirable, and this combine with attendance at training classes, obedience tests and working trials will build up the experience which will enable you fully to utilise your dog's intelligence.

CHAPTER SEVEN

TRACKING

*Finding articles. Advanced tracking hints. Trials and
finding lost persons*

SOME DOGS may have a good nose while others are hopeless,
so the ability of the dog to detect people or objects by scent
will determine the degree to which training for tracking
may be most usefully carried. Only dogs with exceptionally
good noses will be able to carry out the more advanced
tests, because in these exercises, one does not train the dog's
scenting powers but only his ability to co-operate with his
handler in following a track. The laying of a good trail is
affected by quite a number of things, of which atmosphere
and local conditions are not the least important. Successful
tracking is essentially teamwork in which the dog provides
scenting ability and the handler reasoning power and experience. It is the fusion of these attributes of dog and handler which forms the purpose of these exercises, since without
mutual understanding and faith, success will not be possible.

When the dog is tracking, he follows the scent of the
track layer's feet or of objects which have been touched; in
addition to this there may be the freshening of the scent of
grass and earth caused by pressure or disturbance when
being walked over. A small or light person will therefore
leave a fainter trail than a large or heavy one. In fresh tracks,
complications may result from a certain amount of body
scent hanging in the air, more or less over the line, or even
some distance away where it has been carried by movements
of the air. This touches upon the following of wind-borne
scent, which is not, correctly speaking, tracking, but has to

be taken into consideration. So also has the ability of dogs to pick up scent in spite of obstructions, so that it is puzzling to know how it has been detected, or even to pick up airborne scent with the wind blowing away from them.

Hard, dry ground does not hold scent well, and of course busy thoroughfares are almost impossible, but good rich farmland is ideal, provided that the dog has been trained to ignore stock.

The humidity of the air affects the holding of scent in that it improves from very dry to moist air, and may for the latter reason be better in early morning and late evening. However, scent is destroyed by excessive moisture such as rain, frost, thaws or fog. The direction of the wind may help scenting conditions apart from other considerations, in that a dry south wind and not too blowy west wind are best, while north and east winds are unhelpful.

It is hardly fair to the dog to expect him to work properly when he has a cold, constipation, or other ailment of a like nature which tends to dull the sense of smell and the handler would be well advised to consult his vet, or to use some well-tried remedy to give relief to the dog, and not to force him to work until all adverse conditions have been cleared away.

Tracking will best be carried out with the dog wearing a light harness, since a collar is not suitable owing to its throttling and restrictive action under tracking conditions. A leash, about ten yards long should be employed, the actual length used varying according to the conditions.

The dog soon associates the bringing out of the harness and the pleasures which it should signal—an enjoyable track, the praise of its handler, and rewards for work done. There is definitely something wrong with the handler's method of training if the dog does not register pleasurable anticipation when the harness is brought out and strapped on him.

Tracking in an elementary form has already been practised within the exercises in scent discrimination, and only when proficiency has been attained should there be any attempt at the more advanced tracking exercises. An important rule to observe in all tracking, whether in a test or simply carrying out an exercise, is that the dog should *never* "fail". If he fails in a test, he should get as much praise and reward as when the track has been brought to a successful conclusion; during an exercise, and before a fault has had time to bring discouragement, an article impregnated with the same scent should be conveniently "planted" and its discovery hailed with the same pleasure and reward as would have greeted the original. A dog has no reasoning powers or philosophy to overcome disappointments caused by loss of scent and similar troubles, therefore lack of interest is bound to result when trails are lost, and a fruitless search is combined with an impatient handler. As in every other exercise, the game should be carried on only within the capacity of the pupil to maintain interest, and should end in pleasantness and mutual congratulations. Grass holds the scent best, so the early lessons should be given on short grass, well away from any form of distraction and confusion likely to be incurred by the presence of people or animals. When a suitable place has been found, "down" the dog, having shown him and, if necessary, teased him with the article to be used for practice; then walk off, say, forty or fifty feet away and drop the article in full view of the dog, but hidden in the grass so that, while the dog has watched it being dropped, he is unable to see it lying in the grass until almost on top of it. If it is possible to place the dog down-wind while hiding the article, do so, as it will help him to locate it. After having dropped the article, make a circuit and come up to the dog so as not to go over the previous tracks. Then show him the beginning of the trail which was made from the dog to where the article was hidden. Draw the dog's attention to it with the command to "Seek!" Allow the dog to choose his own pace and method of working and do not spoil the whole exercise for him by pushing his nose down on to the trail. With practice the dog will gradually become expert at finding the article, provided that he is correctly started off at the beginning of the "track"; he may be allowed to bring back the article just as in the "Retrieve", or simply bark on discovery.

Friends whom the dog knows may be introduced and the dog allowed to track them, after being shown some article impregnated with their scent, just as in the previous exercises.

Advanced tracking will require considerably more experience in its teaching than the novice is able to impart to his dog, and it is suggested that this fascinating work should be carried further at a training school, or under the direction of a qualified instructor. In a small book, such as this one, there is no space to give a thorough grounding on the theoretical side of the work to supplement practical exercises under expert supervision; therefore only a few brief notes can be given.

It cannot be urged too strongly or too often upon the beginner in dog training that "man-work" is distinct from tracking and the guarding of personal property. In this book we have been concerned with the training of a dog who obediently carries out certain tasks to which he has been trained. The training has always been based upon the fundamental trait in every dog's character that it is good fun and a pleasure to do exactly what his handler wishes him to do and to be allowed to play a number of interesting games with him. A tit-bit or word of praise will be equally gratifying, and one or other reward is sure to be forthcoming whether the game has been successfully concluded or otherwise. Therefore, the dog so trained is a good-natured, happy fellow, not always clever enough to realise the reasons behind some of the actions which he is asked to perform, but sensible and good-natured enough to understand that carry-

Manwork. A Dobermann Pinscher attacking a supposed
criminal

An Alsatian (Loki of Hatherlow) demonstrating the capture of a criminal endeavouring to escape on a bicycle

ing out certain of these puzzling little tasks gives his handler a great deal of pleasure.

Tracking is therefore another task with a happy ending. The dog sees his tracking harness brought out and realises that it is the beginning of another game of following a scent across country or along roads until he finds the person who made it; and who will give him something nice, or rather his handler will give it on his behalf. This is important for the following reason. The average handler will not be likely to have many opportunities to help the police in criminal work, but there will always be the possibility that with a well-trained tracker, he will have opportunities to trace missing persons or articles. The missing person, likely as not, will be a child, and there lies a potential danger. Tracking brings out the latent hunting instinct in a dog, so that certain breeds and partly trained individuals when suddenly confronted by their "quarry" during the course of a tracking run will "pounce" and bite purely through excitement.

Legends to the contrary notwithstanding, a body in the water will still give off scent to a good tracker, so that there is always the chance of discovering the path taken by the track-layer even when he takes to a stream or river; in a number of cases bodies have been found in water through the keen nose of a good tracker. Successful tracking, however, is the result of a working partnership between an experienced handler and his charge, and the handler if he understands his job will know when to help the dog by putting him on the trail at less obvious but probable places or letting the dog work things out for himself. Finding a lost person is very often a different and more difficult proposition in actual fact than when faced with the problem in a test. In the former case, quite a number of people have been over the ground before the dog has had a chance to get to work. Needless to say, the personal scent of the lost

E

person should be given to the dog as strongly as possible, preferably by giving him underwear to smell.

Details have been given elsewhere regarding tracking requirements under test conditions. When searching for a lost person conditions may not always be standard; for instance, the scent may be new, with or without the distraction of people, stock or vehicular traffic; or the scent may be an old one with or without the distractions mentioned. In the majority of cases, the scent will be old with a number of distractions, and the trail may start indoors or outdoors. The handler should study the technique used by experienced trainers in starting their dogs; he will notice that they stay some distance from the starting point and do not make the trail even more confusing. These and a number of other useful tips can be learned at trials and classes, as well as getting used to an experienced tracker who does not appear ever to gallop off at full speed with his nose glued to the ground, but goes off eagerly with head at normal level because as often as not, the scent does not lie actually upon the ground but hangs some distance above it, or may be wind-borne.

By graduated exercises the handler can train the dog to search for hidden objects or lost trails by quartering the ground in a zig-zag, the handler walking straight ahead and indicating to the dog points right or left ahead of him, as he proceeds. This presupposes a thorough grounding in obedience work, upon which all such advanced work is based, because this quartering of the ground is only possible after the dog has become proficient in the "Send away" and "Drop" exercises described previously; only in this instance the dog is not dropped but is sent to points ahead of the handler.

When training for tracking on old or new trails with distractions, use is made of objects handled by the track-layer, which are dropped wherever possible on the trail to serve as markers for handler and dog. Not only should the trail in these exercises cross sheep or cattle tracks, but the handler should endeavour to have the dog practise upon trails which have been traversed recently by stock or people. As proficiency increases, the track-layer should circle or double in order to break the straight line which would be normal during the earlier exercises.

When markers are used, they will show the handler that the dog is following the line, and as each one is reached and identified by the dog, they furnish an excuse to praise him and keep up interest in the game. It should be noted, however, that the dog may not work exactly on top of the trail, and there may be sound reasons for this, so that during tracking, the handler must always be on the alert and apply his own deductive powers.

One of the reasons for the dog not working exactly over the trail could be that the scent has drifted down wind a little since it was laid, another being that the dog is working to windward but parallel to the track. The handler must learn to allow for these and a number of other factors, because the search for a lost person is not always the easy job of being towed along by a clever dog hot on the scent; the handler must always be alert, yet while having confidence in his dog, must be constantly aware of what he is doing, and use his human reasoning powers to help him. In conclusion to these brief notes on tracking may be added this simple hint: when taking the dog to compete in trials or to conduct a search, if there is a considerable car or train journey before you, give him a chance to breathe pure air and thus keep his nose keen, and do not surround him with a fug of tobacco smoke.

CHAPTER EIGHT

HOW DOG TRAINING HAS DEVELOPED

Early training of dogs. Police, Military and A.R.P.
work. In the diamond mines. Guide dogs for the blind

THE USE of dogs for tracking, sentry duty and messenger work goes well back into history, and it would appear that apart from sporting dogs, the training of dogs for specific duties, which are now classified under the general heading of police duties, goes back for several centuries. The early training of dogs was for the purpose of guarding property, protecting their owners and searching for felons or other "wanted" persons, which included tracking. In Scotland, certain classes of people were not allowed to move away from a particular area without permission, this state of affairs continuing up to about a hundred years ago, and runaways were tracked down by bloodhounds, those who refused the hounds access to their land or houses being treated as accomplices. The term "bloodhound", while it did refer to the dog known under that name to-day, also embraced other dogs who were trained for tracking, and their ferocity was often encouraged for the pulling down of their human quarry, which incidentally, the true Bloodhound as we know him, is not likely to be good at, as he is normally a good-natured tracking specialist.

Stock and cattle stealing were carried out to an alarming extent in the Border Country, and in the eighteenth century the farmers and landowners used trained dogs, "bloodhounds" as they were then called, a term which, as explained above, could also include a variety of tracking hounds as well as the Bloodhound proper.

Certain experiments were carried out on the Continent near the end of last century with the result that the Alsatian was chosen as being at that time, the most suitable breed for use in police work. In this country, probably the first use of dogs by our modern police force was by the Wiltshire police in 1912, but trained dogs for guarding depots, etc., were used by our railways considerably earlier than that, most of these dogs being imported from the continent where their invaluable services were early recognised, for military service as well as police work.

Dogs were used in foreign armies as sentries, messengers, and for miscellaneous tasks, but we, in this country, did not encourage or, rather were too blind, to see their value. It was only the faith and persistence of men like Lt.-Col Richardson which broke down the lack of interest of our War Office. During World War I the ability of the Alsatian secured the admiration of his master's enemies, with the result that the cult of the Alsatian, and latterly of dog training has reached unforeseen dimensions in this country.

Practically all properly laid out and equipped training grounds are owned by the Ministry of Supply, the Army, R.A.F. and Police.

A few clubs exist here for training dogs in obedience and police work, but the provision of a proper training ground is beyond the means of most of them. The British Alsatian Association, the Associated Sheep Police and Army Dog Society, and the London and Home Counties Boxer Club are doing good work through their branches in this respect, and owner of all breeds will receive useful advice and help from them. The British Alsatian Association, for example, has realised how handicapped many training classes have been by the lack of trained instructors to take charge of the education of both the dog owners and their dogs. In consequence Training Schools for instructors have recently been opened in London, Birmingham and Cardiff, where practical instruction in the teaching of obedience work is given to the nominees of the various branches of the British Alsatian Association. These schools are being very well attended. It is hoped that they will eventually make available a much higher standard of instruction to a much larger number of dog owners than has previously been possible. The very fact that such schools should be necessary proves how anxious, ready and willing the present-day dog owner is to learn how he can make his dog a well-trained and companionable member of society.

The demonstrations of trained dogs which are frequently given at shows of various descriptions are rather over-dramatised with the result that the average spectator has the impression that the principal duty of a police dog is attacking and mauling criminals, whereas very little indeed of that type of work is necessary, and the dog's teeth are only used under the strictest control. The writer deplores the trend of obedience tests in this country to turn the dog into an automaton, the precision of his performance being everything to some judges, and very little attention being paid to the underlying character and intelligence of the dog.

On the Continent, police work includes the patrolling of frontiers. The long and intensive training to which the dogs are subjected, produces a reliable freelance who is entrusted with an area of country within the beat of his handler. Any person not known to the dog is soon discovered and held up, the attention of the handler being drawn to the "incident" by the barking of the dog. Other recognised activities of police dogs at home and abroad are saving drowning persons, and a variety of tracking, guarding and messenger work.

Military dogs generally had the most difficult duties to perform, such as mine detecting. As a patrol edged forward over the suspected territory, the dog attached to it was on the alert for the buried mines, and would refuse to go forward, as he had been trained, until the mines were found or the patrol skirted the danger spot.

Messenger work is carried out under conditions which test the dog's nerve and reliability, the dog being sent from post to post under fire or during air raids. In addition to the Army, our A.R.P. services used messenger dogs, during raids, also for rescue and Red Cross duties. The messenger dog was invaluable when communications were cut during raids, and the marvellous rescue work performed was hardly believable. The dogs indicated living or dead bodies in wreckage, often under conditions which would have appeared to make correct identification impossible. When Smithfield Meat Market was bombed, living and dead persons and the meat were buried in puzzling confusion until the rescue dogs were set upon the task of detecting human beings from the less urgent animal remains.

The employment of messenger dogs by the police has already been mentioned, their greatest use being in remote country districts, where carrying messages forms part of the general training of the dogs attached to the section, there being of course no necessity for specialisation.

The duties of a guard dog at camps or dumps are to assist the patrol in the detection of intruders and give warning of anything unusual. The dog would be free or on leash, and would have to detect, by scent or hearing, any intruders and where they were hidden. Warning by barking is immediately given and the dog trained to hold, guard, or escort undesirables when found. The dog has to be steady under gun-fire and unhesitatingly protect his handler in the event of attack.

Police dogs are extensively used in the diamond fields. The South African police have had a splendidly organised dog section for many years, using such breeds as Dobermanns, Rottweilers, Rhodesian Ridgebacks, and a cross between the first two breeds mentioned and some other breeds.

The training of these dogs has been brought to perfection by the South African police. Starting from puppyhood, the work covers obedience, climbing, jumping, swimming and tracking.

Quite a number of people are aware of the work of the Guide Dogs for the Blind Association Ltd., but the work is less well known than it deserves to be, and the methods used in training these dogs serve as examples of intelligent study and extreme patience. Some details of these methods will be given, and the novice, or even experienced handler is advised to study in greater detail the system used by the Association. It is also hoped by drawing the attention of readers, that they will show their interest in a practical way and help the movement. The Secretary of the Guide Dogs for the Blind Association Ltd., is Miss Lilian M. Shrimpton, and the address 81 Piccadilly, London, W.1. The Association is a purely voluntary organisation, depending upon public support to provide funds for its work. St. Dunstan's, the National Institute for the Blind, various trusts and other organisations which help charity work support it within their means.

The Guide Dogs for the Blind has been working for nearly twenty years in this country, starting from the very bottom, without money and without much support from the public. Being new its usefulness was doubted. The struggle for existence remains, but the Association has gained ground, sympathy towards the movement has increased, and the general knowledge of the usefulness of a guide dog has spread widely.

The remarkable work carried out by the Association's trainer, Captain N. Liakhoff, the ex-Tsarist officer, first at Wallasey and now at Leamington Spa and Exeter, has completely revolutionised the lives of many blind persons.

It costs over £200 to train a guide dog and his blind owner, a sum usually beyond the capacity of most blind people to pay. Many blind people pay a small part of the cost of the dog themselves, but if they cannot, they are provided with a dog at a nominal cost. It takes four months to teach a dog his duties by methods advanced by Captain Liakhoff after long and patient study of canine behaviour. The dog must be large, so as to move in harmony with a human being; a small one would accelerate too quickly. The principal breeds used are Alsatians, Collies of different varieties, Retrievers of various kinds, and Boxers. The dog is taught the meaning of four basic commands—"Forward!", "Stop!", "Right!" and "Left!"—but he must also learn to disregard these orders if traffic or obstructions are in the way. He learns to stop at all kerbs and always to cross roads at right angles.

Only about 25 per cent of dogs who are sent on approval to the training school are accepted, after receiving most careful temperament tests. The idea which must be introduced to the dog's brain is that he and his master represent, while working, one inseparable whole, and, therefore, the speed of the unit, the size of the unit, the height of the unit are not the speed, size and height of man *or* dog, but those of man *and* dog as one. For instance, it is useless to try to pass through a narrow place where there is room for only one part; a place must be found where the whole can pass safely; or to dash across the road in front of a motor-car with the speed of which only one-half is capable. The introduction of this idea to the dog must be gentle and very gradual. A potential guide dog must like his work, must do it with pleasure; otherwise he cannot be a guide dog.

The trainer starts to walk with his dog, having him on the leash, and puts the harness on only when the dog already knows more or less what he ought to do, to walk in the middle of the pavement, avoid obstacles, stop at kerbs, etc.

The trainer begins with his dog as a seeing man, but gradually simulates losing his sight as the dog's training progresses. When the training of the dog is complete, in the dog's understanding, his master is totally blind.

When the education of the dog is completed, his future master arrives at the training centre to stay for a period of about a month, since a trained dog cannot be used by someone who does not know how to work him. The first few days are taken up in teaching the blind man as much as possible how to give the commands, how to follow his dog, how to feel the dog's movements through the harness and what these movements mean. The knowledge of the differently-shaped kerbs, the different angles of the streets and how to deal with these is given in theoretical lessons and about one hour a day is taken up in walking with the dog. The walk is changed every day in order to give the blind man as much variety as possible. The guide dog leads his master, being connected with him by a special harness which is constructed in such a way that every movement of the dog is felt by his master, whether it is a slight increase or decrease of the rate of progress, or slight variations of direction.

On arriving at each kerb the dog stops, so that his master may know where the kerb is, and also to give a pause before crossing the road. When the master wants to cross he gives the command "Forward!"; if he wants to turn right or left he gives the command accordingly. On every kerb the dog will stop and will wait for the command.

If there is any obstruction on the pavement, the dog will go into the road and back to the pavement again after the obstruction is passed, stopping each time when his master must go down or up the kerb.

If the dog has received the order to cross the road and it is not safe to do so, the dog disobeys the order and does not leave the pavement until the road is clear. If the dog meets traffic while crossing, he will stop and wait, carrying on without any command when the way is clear again. There must not be any diagonal crossing or short cuts. Every

crossing is done at a straight angle to the pavement, so that
the dog is able to watch the traffic from both sides. If the
master wants to cross the road before he arrives at a corner
he gives the dog the command "Stop!" and then the direction
towards the street whether right or left. Then "Forward!"
again to cross the road. So the dog knows four commands:
"Forward!", "Right!", "Left!" and "Stop!" With these four
commands the dog and the man can travel everywhere in
town or country, in known district or unknown, with perfect ease and safety. In his own town or district, which he
knowns, the man does not need to make any enquiries; in
the unknown place or town, to get from one place to another
he must know how many crossings and turnings he has to
make, and would make enquiries from passers-by as a
sighted person would.

A guide dog who has been with his master for a time
usually knows the places which his master visits more or
less frequently. In this case the dog does not receive any
command of direction, only the word which indicates to
him the required destination. Besides this, the dog is trained
to pick up objects which his master may drop.

A blind man who uses a guide dog does not use a stick.
He has his dog on his left-hand side, holding the harness
with the left hand and having his right hand free.

CHAPTER NINE

RULES FOR WORKING TRIALS

*Championship Working Trials – Junior, Senior
"A" and "B" and Open*

By COURTESY of the Associated Sheep, Police and Army Dog Society, the following extracts from their schedules of championship working trials are given. Study of these extracts will give a number of practical hints upon the conditions under which trials are conducted. To be particularly noted by the novice is the explanation of the required working given under each test.

Schedule for Championship Working Trials (T.D.)
Open Stakes and Senior "B", Junior Stakes

REGULATIONS

1. The Trials will be held under the working trials rules and regulations of the Kennel Club as in force at the date of publication of this Schedule.

2. *Entries.* All entries must be received not later than (post mark) . . .

3. *Entry Fees.* The entry fee for each dog for each stake in which it is entered shall be: JUNIOR AND SENIOR B. . . . . OPEN STAKES. . . . Entry fees must be forwarded to the secretary with the entry forms on or before . . . postmark or the entry will not be accepted.

4. *Power to refuse entries or cancel stakes.* The committee reserve to themselves the right to refuse any entries that they may think fit to exclude. In the event of insufficient entries being received the committee reserve the right to cancel any one or more stakes.

5. *Judges.* Should any of the judges be prevented from fulfilling his engagement, or any unforeseen circumstances arise, the

committee reserve the right to appoint another judge or judges in his or her place, and to make any other arrangements that may be deemed necessary.

6. *Judging.* The Meet on . . . will be held. . . . Judging will commence as early as possible after the Meets. The Senior "B" and the Junior and Part I of the Open will be judged on. . . .

7. *Order of Running.* A draw will take place on . . . to determine the order in which the dogs shall compete, and will be drawn by two members of the committee.

8. *Conduct of Handlers.* All handlers must obey the orders of the judges and must bring their dogs forward to be tried immediately they are requested to do so. In the absence of instructions to the contrary, handlers may work their dogs from any position they may choose.

9. *Power to Exclude or Disqualify Dogs.* The judges are empowered to disqualify the dog of any handler who disobeys their orders or interferes with the work of any other competing dog. The judges are empowered to exclude any dog which, in their opinion, is not in a fit condition to compete. Bitches on heat will not be allowed to compete and must be removed from the ground. The entry fee of any dog disqualified will be forfeited.

10. *Owner's Liability.* Owners must accept full liability for any injury to persons or property caused by their dogs, and entries are accepted on the basis of owners indemnifying the Club and its officers against all claims in respect thereof.

11. *Qualifying Certificates.* The judges will be empowered to award Qualifying Certificates. The performance of the dogs will be judged on points. To obtain a TRACKING DOG Certificate a dog must secure 70 per cent of the maximum points in the Open Stakes. A dog securing 70 per cent but less than 75 per cent of maximum points will receive a Certificate with the qualification "GOOD"; 75 per cent but less than 80 per cent with the qualification "VERY GOOD"; and 80 per cent and more with the qualification "EXCELLENT".

To obtain the "COMPANION DOG" Certificate a dog must secure at least 70 per cent of the maximum points in Senior "B" Stakes; 75 per cent but less than 80 per cent secures the Certificate with the qualification "VERY GOOD"; and 80 per cent and more secures the qualification "EXCELLENT".

To obtain the Certificate of Merit for General Obedience in the Junior Stakes, a dog must secure at least 80 per cent of maximum points in the complete schedule of tests and not less than 50 per cent of the points for any individual exercise.

The A.S.P.A.D.S. Certificates of Merit are awarded to dogs belonging to Members only.

12. *Working Trials Championship.* The winner in the Open Stakes must secure at least 80 per cent of the maximum points in order to count towards a working trials championship under Kennel Club working trials rules. It is not now necessary for a specified number of runners to compete in order to count towards the working trials champion.

13. *Appliances.* COLLARS. Plain leather or chain slip collars will be allowed, BUT TRAINING OR SPIKED COLLARS MUST NOT BE USED.

DUMB-BELLS. In the retrieving tests owners may use their own dumb-bells.

LEADS. The lead to be used in "Following at heel" shall be three feet long and held at the free end so that it hangs loosely between dog and handler. Tracking leads shall be of a minimum length of twelve yards.

14. Upon any case or matter arising not provided for in these regulations the committee shall decide thereon.

15. *Alterations in Schedule.* All announcements, prior to the date of closing of entries, in the Kennel Gazette, Our Dogs, and The Field, or any of them, of any alterations made by the committee in the schedule or in these regulations shall be deemed sufficient notice thereof.

16. Judges are particularly requested to remember that spiked or training collars are forbidden; and that any rough handling either during or at the completion of any exercise must be severely penalised.

17. No alteration in the order of tracking is allowed after the draw, except by special permission from the secretary.

18. Instructions relating to Long Jump. This applies to all Stakes. Handlers are permitted to take their dogs up to the first board, without penalty, but must not pass it, neither may they encourage their dogs by throwing any article whatsoever, otherwise the jump will be void.

DEFINITION OF STAKES

Junior Stakes. For dogs and bitches which have never won a

First Prize in Junior Stakes or a First, Second or Third prize in Senior "B", Senior "A" or Open Stakes.

Senior "B" Stakes. For dogs and bitches which have never won a First, Second or Third Prize with the qualification "EXCELENT" in an Open Stake or a First Prize with the qualification "EXCELENT" in a Senior "A" Stake.

Elimination Tests for Open Stakes

If dogs have gained 50 per cent marks on a Senior "A" track, no test is necessary. In other cases handlers wishing to enter for Open Stakes should contact their branch secretary who will arrange to have dogs tested before entries close. Where on account of distance this is impossible, handlers should furnish the Trials Sub-Committee, through the secretary, with proof that their dog can complete a Senior "A" track satisfactorily.

SCHEDULE
JUNIOR STAKES
General Obedience Only

Tests: Points

1. "Heel on leash."   10

   On the handler's command "Heel!", the dog should follow as closely as possible to the left knee of the handler, who should walk smartly in his normal and natural manner. Any tightening or jerking of the leash, or any act, signal or command which in the opinion of the judges, gives the dog unnecessary or unfair assist-ance, shall be penalised. The exercise shall consist of "left turns", "right turns", "about turns", and march-ing in the "figure of eight" at normal walking pace between objects or people two yards apart. The judge may, at his discretion, test also at a fast or very slow pace.

2. "Heel", free.   20

   This should be executed as in No. 1, except that the dog is off the leash.

3. "Sit" (two minutes).   20

   The dog shall sit for the full period of two minutes, all the handlers being out of sight, or as far as possible from the dogs, at the judge's discretion. On the handlers return to their dogs, the latter should not move from the sitting position until the judge's permission has been given. All dogs shall be tested together, sufficient stewards being detailed to assist. The judge may cause the dogs to be tested by sending stewards to walk among them during the exercise.

4. "Drop on Recall" on order from judge to handler. .. 30
This should be executed as in No. 5, except that during the recall the dog should be dropped on order from judge to handler. The dog should drop instantly and remain down until the judge instructs the handler to call his dog up.

5. "Recall to Handler". 15
The dog should be recalled from the "Down" or sitting position, the handler being as far as possible from the dog at the discretion of the judge. The dog should return at a smart pace and sit in front of the handler, afterwards going smartly to heel on command or signal: handler to await command of the judge.

6. Retrieving a dumb-bell not exceeding 2½ lb. on the flat. 20
The dog shall not move forward to retrieve nor deliver to hand on return until ordered by the handler on the judge's instructions. The retrieve should be executed at a fast trot or gallop without mouthing or playing with the object. After delivery the dog goes to heel as in No. 5.

7. Either of the following two exercises at the handler's option: 50

   (a) *Retrieving a dumb-bell not exceeding 10 oz. over 4-ft. jump.*
   Retrieving to be executed as in No. 6, except that the dog must jump the obstacle both going and returning.

   (b) *Sending the dog away not less than twenty paces, and dropping on order from judge to handler.*
   The dog should drop instantly and remain down until the judge instructs the handler to call his dog up.

8. "Down" ten minutes, handlers out of sight. 50
The dogs are to remain in the lying down position for the full period specified, the handlers being out of sight until ordered to return by the judge. The dogs should not

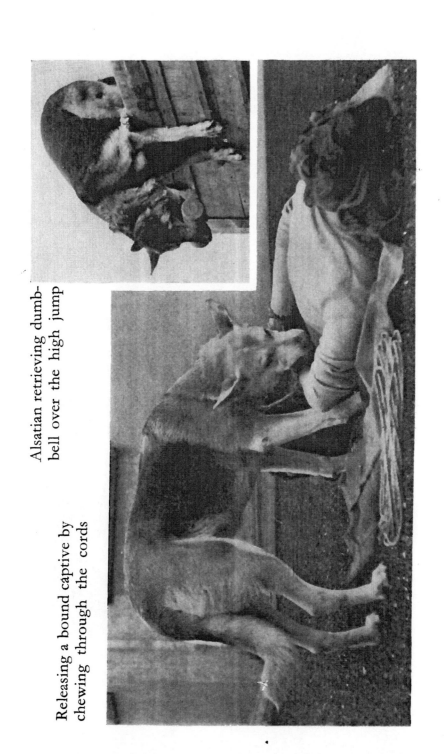

Alsatian retrieving dumb-bell over the high jump

Releasing a bound captive by chewing through the cords

A group of trained Dobermann Pinschers

51

rise from the "down" position until the judge declares the test complete. All dogs in the class or stake should be "down" together, sufficient stewards being detailed to assist. The judge may cause the dogs to be tested by sending stewards to walk among them during the exercise.

215

OPEN STAKES
(For obtaining the qualification "T.D.")

Part 1. *GENERAL OBEDIENCE.* To be executed as indicated in Junior Stakes Schedule

Tests:	Points
1. "Heel on leash"	10
2. "Heel" free	20
3. "Sit" (two minutes)	20
4. Sending dog away, not less than twenty paces, and dropping on order from judge to handler	30
5. "Recall to handler"	15
6. Retrieving dumb-bell not exceeding 2½ lb. on the flat	20
7. Retrieving dumb-bell not exceeding 10 oz. over 6-ft. standard obstacle	50
8. Long Jump (9 ft.)	30
9. "Down", ten minutes; handler out of sight	50

245

Part 2. *CHARACTER OBSERVATION*

Tests:	Points
1. The behaviour of the dogs will be observed generally throughout the duration of the trials, both on and off the leash, and amongst people with and without dogs, with a view to an assurance that no dog of a nervous or vicious nature can obtain a Working Trials Championship or Certificate of Merit.	60
2. Food Tests.	20

This test shall be submitted while the dog is off the leash. It shall not be submitted during other exercises.

F

3. Speaking on command and ceasing to bark when the handler is ordered by the judge.   25

                                                                        105
                                                                        ──

Part 3. *TRACKING*

1. "Seek back", not less than two hundred yards, but a longer distance if available, for handler's article.   50
The article used, which must not be a conspicuous one nor a handkerchief, to be approved by the judge. The article to be dropped surreptitiously by the handler after he has proceeded at least 30 paces.

2. "Leash track"; approximately one mile long, but not less than seven furlongs: scent two hours old; two articles dropped by the track-layer to be found, one about the middle and one at the end of the track; stranger's scent; an article to be left at the commencement of the track by the track-layer.   575
The tracks shall be plotted on the ground by the stewards on the day previous to the tracking meeting, if possible. The track-layers shall then follow the plotted track, deposit the articles to be found at the commencement, the middle and end of the track, and return in a single line, one peg not more than 30 yards from the commencement of the track to be left in to indicate the direction of the track. The cross track should be approximately $\frac{1}{4}$ hour old. The crossing should be made at two points, approximately half and two-thirds of the distance from the commencement of the track. The stewards should indicate the crossing points on each track with larger stakes which shall be picked up by the layers of cross track.

3. "Free Track"; approximately 400 yards long; not necessarily in a straight line; $\frac{1}{4}$ hour old   75
The dog is to be given a heel mark of the track-layer   125
and then to discriminate track-layer's article at the end of the track from other stranger's articles, of a similar nature to the track-layer's, such articles to be scattered over the last 30 yards of the track. The dog to return with the article to handler.

Schedule for CH. Working Trials (P.D.)
Open Stakes and Senior "A" & "B", Junior Stakes

The Regulations are as previously given, but the following definition of stakes should be noted:

Senior "A" Stakes. For dogs and bitches which have never won a First, Second or Third Prize with the qualification "EXCELLENT" in an Open Stake.

Open Stakes. P.D. Open Stakes are confined to the following breeds: Alsatians, Bullmastiffs, Dobermann Pinschers, Staffordshire Bull Terriers, Bull Terriers, Airedale Terriers, Boxers, Rhodesian Ridgebacks, Rottweilers, Retrievers, Standard Poodles, Groenendaels, Collies (Rough and Smooth), Great Danes and Schnauzers.

SENIOR "A" STAKES
(For obtaining the qualification "U.D.")

Tests:	Points
1. "Heel on leash"	10
2. "Heel", free	20
3. "Sit" (two minutes)	20
4. Sending dog away, not less than twenty paces, and dropping on order from judge to handler	50
5. "Recall to handler"	15
6. Retrieving dumb-bell not exceeding 2½ lb. on the flat	20
7. For dogs not exceeding 15 in. at the shoulder, retrieve a 10-oz. dumb-bell over a 4-ft. standard article	50
8. Long jump 6 ft. for dogs not exceeding 15 in. at the shoulder. Long jump 9 ft. for dogs exceeding 15 in. at the shoulder.	30
9. "Down", 10 minutes; handlers out of sight	50
10. "Seek back", 100 yds., handler's article	30
11. Scent discrimination on judge's article, handler's scent	50
12. "Leash track", not less than ½-mile long and at least ½-hour old, on stranger's scent	250
	595

SENIOR "B" STAKES
(For obtaining the qualification "C.D.")

TESTS:	Points
1. "Heel on leash"	10
2. "Heel", free	20
3. "Sit" (two minutes)	20
4. Sending dog away, not less than 20 paces, and dropping on order from judge to handler	50
5. "Recall to handler"	15
6. Retrieving dumb-bell on the flat	20
7. For dogs not exceeding 15 in. at the shoulder retrieve a 10-oz. dumb-bell over a 4-ft. standard obstacle. For dogs exceeding 15 in. at the shoulder retrieve a 10-oz. dumb-bell over a 6-ft. standard obstacle	50
8. Long jump 6 ft. for dogs not exceeding 15 in. at the shoulder. Long jump 9 ft. for dogs exceeding 15 in. at the shoulder	30
9. "Down" 10 minutes: handlers out of sight	50
10. Scent discrimination on judge's article, handler's scent	50
	315

N.B. Where dogs are entered in BOTH Senior "A" and Senior "B" Stakes, they will not be required to go through the tests twice, except by the handler's express wish. The markings for the tests in Senior "B" would be the same as those obtained in the corresponding tests in Senior "A"

OPEN STAKES
(For obtaining the qualification "T.D.")

Part 1. *GENERAL OBEDIENCE*. To be executed as indicated in Junior Stakes Schedule

TESTS:	Points
1. "Heel on leash"	10
2. "Heel", free ..	20
3. "Sit" (two minutes)	20
4. Sending dog away, not less than 20 paces, and dropping on order from judge to handler	50
5. "Recall to handler"	15

6. Retrieving dumb-bell not exceeding 2½ lb. on the flat   20
7. Retrieving dumb-bell not exceeding 10 oz. over 6-ft.
   standard obstacle   50
8. Long jump (9 ft.)   30
9. "Down", 15 minutes; handlers out of sight   50

                                                                 ———
                                                                 265
                                                                 ———

Part 2. *TRACKING AND SCENT TESTS*

10. "Seek back" not less than 100 yards for handler's
    article   30
    The article used, which must not be a conspicuous one,
    nor a handkerchief, to be approved by the judge. The
    article to be dropped surreptitiously by the handler
    after he has proceeded at least 30 paces
11. Scent discrimination on article provided by the judge.
    Handler's scent   50
    A separate similar article to be used for each dog. This
    exercise is to follow the "Down!" Article to be given
    to handler as he leaves the ring for the "Down" and to
    be collected on re-entering the ring. Article must not
    be given to the dog.
12. "Leash track", not less than ⅓ mile long and at least ½-
    hour old, on stranger's scent, track-layer's article to
    be left at the end of track   250
    The tracks shall be plotted on the ground by the
    stewards on the day previous to the track meeting, if
    possible. One peg not more than 30 yards from the
    commencement of the track will be left in to indicate
    direction of the track.

                                                                 ———
                                                                 330
                                                                 ———

Part 3. *DEFENCE WORK*

13. *Refusal of food*   20
    This test shall be submitted whilst the dog is off the
    leash but not in conjunction with any other exercise.
14. *Guarding* (dog attached)   50
    It is sufficient if the dog shows to the satisfaction of the

judge, that he is protecting the object to be guarded but he should not attack or attempt to attack a casual passer-by.

15. Quartering the ground for hidden "criminal", and baying but not biting when found.   70
16. Stick and gun sureness   60
17. Search and escort of criminal. Defending handler when attacked and immediate release when attack ceases   100
18. Guarding "criminal" in handler's absence. The dog is not to attack until the "criminal" threatens him or endeavours to escape. Dog to release man when he halts   50
19. Recall from "criminal" running away   50

                                                                                                        ────
                                                                                                        400
                                                                                                        ────

Note on Tests 5 to 20.

The dog should not be brought on to the trials ground until the "criminal" has been concealed. A steward should be so placed that he can observe whether the dog bites the "criminal" on his discovery. The dog should quarter the ground well in accordance with direction given by the judge. When the "criminal" has been found and the judge and handler have come up, the dog should be tested with both gun and stick, after which the "criminal" is searched and disarmed and then escorted by handler and dog. During the escort the "criminal" will attack the handler, when the dog should immediately defend his master, but release the "criminal" immediately the latter ceases to attack, and stand still. The dog will be judged on his escort work during the execution of the whole of this section. He will be placed to guard the "criminal" whilst his handler is absent but he should make no attempt to attack unless the "criminal" threatens him or endeavours to escape. The dog's attacks should always cease immediately the "criminal" ceases to threaten him or to move. During the escort, the "criminal" will surreptitiously drop an article (not revolver nor an article belonging to the handler or owner of the dog), which should on command be retrieved and brought to hand by the dog. In the final test (19) the dog is sent after the escaping "criminal" but is recalled before reaching him. The dog should be going at a good speed when recalled. It is permissible for the handler to "Drop" or "Down" his dog before recalling.

During the execution of this section, the handler is permitted to give commands or signals to his dog excepting in Test 18. Repetition of commands or signals is a fault which should be penalised.

Every unnecessary bite will be heavily penalised.

NOTE: Details of Junior Stake Tests for these trials are as given previously.

CHAPTER TEN

OBEDIENCE TESTS AND TRIALS

Kennel Club Regulations. American Kennel Club Regulations

A FEW notes on obedience tests and working trials may prove helpful to the novice, together with some details of the present regulations. Obedience tests are now being increasingly included in the schedules of dog shows, but for more severe and practical tests, entries should be made in working trials which are held in the open and under working conditions. In these trials three tests are usually provided, each consisting of various exercises, graded to suit the novice and the more experienced handler. The method of judging is by the award of marks for each exercise. Careful study should be given to the number of points awarded for the correct performance of the exercise: it will be observed that some rate more highly than others, so an effort must be made to secure as many as possible of these valuable points by concentrating upon the particular exercise carrying the largest number of points. In practice, the method of assessing merit is not to build up the score, but to take the maximum, reducing it by disallowing points as penalties for faults. Under certain circumstances a handler will have to observe fine judgment in deciding the particular type of fault for which he is willing to be penalised, should he be working a dog which is weak on certain exercises. Should he invite the penalty for repeating the order, or allow the dog to fault? Only a thorough knowledge of the system of points valuation of each exercise will enable the handler to decide quickly and correctly, should the emergency arise.

It is suggested that the novice should start with the obedience test, then enter for the Junior Stakes in the working trials, thence graduate through Senior B. Stakes, A Stakes and finally enter for Open Stakes, taking either "Police Dog" or "Tracking Dog", according to inclination for the work.

By joining one of the numerous local branches of the British Alsatian Association, or A.S.P.A.D.S., many opportunities to test out a dog are afforded at one or other of many matches regularly arranged. The best way to pick up the technique of handling a dog in the various competitions is to attend as many trials as possible, study the rules thoroughly, watch carefully, and reason out the methods of handling adopted by the experienced exhibitors.

Many of the hints given on ringcraft also hold good for work in obedience tests and working trials.

The dog should be accustomed to working in strange surroundings, so change the location of the practice exercise frequently. Don't forget to take all the apparatus to be used in the trials—leash, collars, dumb-bell, articles for scent discrimination, etc.

Don't overfeed the dog on competition day; keep the heavy meal until after the work is finished for the day. Above all, be punctual in arriving at the Meet and in coming up for your class. Avoid "bribing" the dog with dainties; he will soon learn to live on praise alone on competition days, and this gives a better impression to judge and spectators.

If the handler is a good sportsman, the chances are that it is infectious: the combined exhibition of dog and handler will be a pleasure to watch.

The Rules and Regulations for Obedience Classes and Working Trials are reproduced by courtesy of the Kennel Club.

KENNEL CLUB REGULATIONS FOR TESTS
FOR OBEDIENCE CLASSES

1. Kennel Club Show Regulations shall where applicable and as amended or varied from time to time apply to Obedience Tests as follows:

Kennel Club Championship Show Regulations	to Championship Obedience Shows.
Kennel Club Licence Show Regulations	to Licence Obedience Shows.
Kennel Club Regulations for Sanction Shows	to Sanction Obedience Shows.

2. No deviation from the following Tests can be entertained and any or all of the following classes may be scheduled.

Tests may be placed in any order in the Schedule but this order must be followed at the Show.

In all these tests the handler may use the dog's name with a command or signal without penalty.

In all the following Definitions of Tests First Prize wins at Limited and Sanction Show Obedience Tests will not count when entering for Open and Championship Obedience Tests.

In Novice, Test "A" and Test "B" handlers may use their own dumb-bells.

In composite exercises and the Sit and Down the points will be graduated.

All exercises must include a finish.

Special Beginners. For handlers and dogs that have not won a First Prize in an Obedience Test or Championship Working Trials.

Handlers will not be penalised for encouragement or extra commands except in the Sit and Down. In these Tests, at the discretion of the judge, handlers may face their dogs.

1. Heel on Lead, 15 points; 2. Heel Free, 20 points; 3. Sit One Minute, handler in sight, 10 points; 4. Down Two Minutes, handler in sight, 20 points; 5. Recall from Sit or Down, position at handler's choice. Dog to be recalled by handler when stationary, sit in front, go to heel—all on command of judge to handler. Distance at discretion of judge. Exercise commences when

handler leaves dog on judge's command, 10 points; 6. Retrieve any Article provided by handler, 25 points. TOTAL: 100 points.

Novice. For dogs that have not won a First Prize in an Obedience Test (Special Beginners excepted) or Championship Working Trials.

Handlers will not be penalised for encouragement or extra commands except in the Sit and Down. In these Tests, at the discretion of the judge, handlers may face their dogs.

Exercises and points in Nos. 1 to 5 same as Special Beginners. 6. Retrieve a Dumb-Bell, 25 points. TOTAL :100 points.

Test A, Undergraduate. For dogs that have not won four First Prizes in Obedience Tests (Special Beginners and Novice excepted) or Championship Working Trials.

Simultaneous command and signal will be permitted. Extra commands or signals will be penalised.

1. Heel on Lead, 20 points; 2. Heel Free, 20 points; 3. Sit One Minute, handler in sight, 10 points; 4. Recall from Sit or Down, position at handler's choice. Dog to be recalled to heel by handler, on command of judge, whilst handler is walking away, both to continue forward. Exercise commences when handler leaves dog on judge's command, 10 points; 5. Retrieve a Dumb-Bell, 25 points; 6. Down Five Minutes, handler out of sight, 30 points; 7. Scent Discrimination, handler's scent on handler's article. Unsuitable articles may be rejected at the discretion of the judge, 30 points. TOTAL: 145 points.

Test B, Graduate. Obedience Champions are not eligible for Test B.

AT MEMBERS' SHOWS. For Dogs that have not won four First Prizes in Test "B" Graduate, Test "C" Open or Championship Working Trials.

AT OPEN AND CHAMPIONSHIP SHOWS. For dogs that have not won four First Prizes in Obedience Tests or Championship Working Trials. Wins in Special Beginners, Novice, Test "A", and any Test at Members' Shows excepted.

One command, by word or signal, except in Ex. 4. Extra commands or signals will be penalised.

1. Heel on Lead, 20 points; 2. Heel Free, 20 points; 3. Sit Two Minutes, handler out of sight, 20 points; 4. Send Away, Drop and Recall. On command of judge to handler, dog to be sent away in direction indicated by judge. After the dog has been

dropped handler will call the dog to heel whilst walking where directed by judge and both will continue forward. No obstacle to be placed in path of dog. Simultaneous command and signal permitted in send away but as soon as the dog leaves the handler the arm must be dropped, 40 points; 5. Retrieve a Dumb-Bell, 25 points; 6. Stand One Minute, handler at least ten paces away, 10 points; 7. Down Ten Minutes, handler out of sight, 50 points; 8. Scent Discrimination, handler's scent on article provided by judge. A separate similar article to be used for each dog. This exercise to follow the "Down". Article to be given to the handler as he leaves the ring for the "Down". No points will be awarded if the article is given to the dog, 40 points. TOTAL: 225 points.

Test C, Open. One command, by word or signal, except in exercise. 3. Extra commands or signals will be penalised.

1. Heel Free, including fast and slow. Figure 8 may be included at judge's discretion, 40 points; 2. Sit Two Minutes, handler out of sight, 20 points; 3. Send Away, Drop and Recall, as in Test B, 40 points; 4. Retrieve Any One Article which must not be in any manner injurious to the dog (definitely excluding food or glass). The article to be picked up easily by any breed of dog and clearly visible to the dog. A separate similar article to be used for each dog, 30 points; 5. Down Ten Minutes, handler out of sight, 50 points; 6. Scent Discrimination, judge's scent on piece of material not less than 6 in. by 6 in. provided by judge. A separate similar piece to be used for each dog. Method of taking scent at handler's choice, 50 points; 7. Distant Control. Dog to sit, stand and down, in one place not less than ten paces from handler, in any order on command from judge to handler. Six instructions to be given in the same order for each dog. Excessive movement in any direction by the dog, having regard to its size, will be penalised, 50 points; 8. Advanced Stand, Sit and Down. Handler to walk with dog at heel free, leave dog standing (sitting or down) when judge commands and continues forward alone without hesitation round the ring until he reaches dog, both then continue forward, when other positions will follow in a similar manner. Order of positions (same for each dog) at judge's discretion, 40 points. TOTAL: 320 points.

Additional Exercise. Which may be included at open-air Shows where conditions are satisfactory; 9. Seek Back (Dog to seek flat inconspicuous article, minimum ten paces. Dog must walk at

heel, walk will include left and right turns. Time limit, 5 minutes),
40 points.

3. The Kennel Club will offer an Obedience Certificate Dog
and an Obedience Certificate Bitch for winners of First Prizes
in Test "C" Dog and Test "C" Bitch at a Championship Show,
provided that the exhibits do not lose more than 10 points out
of 320, and provided also that the Tests are open to all breeds.

The Kennel Club will offer at Cruft's Dog Show each year
the Kennel Club Obedience Championship—Dog and the Kennel Club Obedience Championship—Bitch. The dogs entitled to
compete are those awarded Obedience Certificates during the
year preceding Cruft's Show.

The Tests for the Championships shall be those required for
Test "C" Open in these Regulations. If the winning dog or bitch
has lost more than 10 points out of 320, the Championship award
shall be withheld.

4. The following dogs shall be entitled to be described as
Obedience Champions and shall receive a Certificate to that effect
from the Kennel Club:

(a) The winners of the Kennel Club Obedience Championships.

(b) A dog awarded three Obedience Certificates under three
different judges in accordance with these Regulations.

5. Spayed bitches and castrated dogs are permitted to compete
in Obedience Tests.

Extract from Kennel Club Working Trial Rules and Regulations
Working Trials are divided into three categories:
(a) Championships; (b) Open; (c) Members.

1. *Management of Working Trial Meetings.* The management of
a meeting shall be entrusted to not less than three Field Stewards
who shall be appointed by the committee of the society holding
the trial.

Any disputed matter requiring a decision on the ground shall
be decided by the stewards and the judges.

Any event at a Working Trial not provided for in these Rules
and Regulations shall be decided by a majority of stewards of the
meeting, assisted by the judges, and their decision shall be final.

2. *Judges.* When a judge, from ill-health, or any other unexpected cause, is prevented from attending or finishing a meeting, the stewards shall have the power of deciding what action is
to be taken.

3. *Schedule.* A Society holding a Working Trial must issue a schedule which is to be treated as a contract between the Society and the public and neither party is permitted to make any modification before the date of the Trial except by advertising in suitable papers before the closing of entries, and such modification must be immediately notified in writing to the Kennel Club.

The schedule must contain:

(a) The date and place of the Working Trial.

(b) The latest date for applying for entry at the Trial.

(c) The amounts of entry fees and all prize money.

(d) The conditions and the date of the draw to determine the order in which the dogs shall be run in tracking tests.

(e) The conditions and qualifications for making entries and for intimating acceptance or refusal of entries.
P.D. Open Stakes are confined to the following breeds—Alsatians, Bullmastiffs, Dobermann Pinschers, Staffordshire Bull Terriers, Bull Terriers, Airedale Terriers, Boxers, Rhodesian Ridgebacks, Rottweilers, Retrievers, Standard Poodles, Groenendaels, Collies (Rough and Smooth), Great Danes and Schnauzers.

(f) An announcement that the Working Trial is held under these Rules and Regulations with such exceptions and conditions as the committee of the Society may decide, such exceptions and conditions having previously received the approval of the committee of the Kennel Club.

(g) The definition of each stake together with the qualifications or limitations for each entry in that stake.

(h) The names of judges.

4. *Stewards to determine Weather Conditions.* If a majority of the stewards considers the weather unfit for holding the trials, the meeting may be postponed from day to day until the end of the week, when the stakes that are not decided may be abandoned, and the entry fees returned; or a fresh draw may be arranged, and a fresh date fixed for the meeting.

5. *Handling or Dogs by Owner of his Deputy.* An owner, his keeper, or deputy, may handle the dog, but it must be one or the other; and once the dogs are down, an owner must not interfere with his dog if he has deputed another person to handle him.

6. *Control of Matters Connected with Dogs under Trial.* The control of all matters connected with the dogs under trial shall rest with the judge or judges of the meeting, but they may call the stewards to their assistance if they think fit.

7. *Disqualification of Dogs.* Should any dog be considered by the judges of a meeting unfit to compete by reason of sexual causes, or having any contagious disease, or any cause which clearly interferes with the safety or chance of winning of his opponent, such dog shall be disqualified and removed from the ground.

8. *Certificates.* The judge or judges shall be empowered to give certificates at a Championhip Working Trial; P.D. (Police Dog); U.D. (Utility Dog); T.D. (Tracking Dog); and C.D. (Companion Dog) with the qualifications "Excellent", "Very Good", or "Good", to the prize winners and other dogs. A dog shall not obtain a certificate and the qualification "Excellent" unless it has obtained at least 80 per cent of the maximum points in the appropriate stakes. A dog shall not obtain a certificate and the qualification "Very Good" unless it has obtained at least 75 per cent of the maximum points in the appropriate stakes. A dog shall not obtain a certificate with the qualification "Good" unless it has obtained at least 70 per cent of the maximum points in the appropriate stakes.

The committee of any Working Trial shall be empowered to offer certificates of merit providing the certificates and the conditions of their award have been approved by the committee of the Kennel Club.

9. *Penalties for Impugning the Decisions of the Judges.* If any one taking part in the trials openly impugns the decisions of the judge or judges, he is liable to be dealt with by the committee under the Kennel Club Working Trial Rules 9 or 10.

10. *Judges are Empowered and Instructed to Withhold Prizes where Dogs do not show Sufficient Merit.* The judge or judges will be empowered and instructed to withhold any prize, prizes or certificates if, in his or their opinion, the dogs competing do not show sufficient merit.

11. *Order of Running.* The draw for the order of running in tracking tests shall be made after the tracks have been laid.

12. *Disqualification for Absence.* The committee shall announce the hour for beginning each day, and each dog must be brought

up in its proper turn without delay. If absent when called, the dog shall be liable to be disqualified by the judge or judges.

13. *Method of Working.* The committee may arrange for dogs to be worked singly or together in any numbers. All dogs entered in one stake shall be tested as far as possible under similar conditions.

14. *Regulations regarding Handling.* A person handling a dog may speak, whistle or work him by hand as he thinks proper, but he can be called to order by the judge or judges for making unnecessary noise, and if he persists in doing so, the judge or judges can order the dog to be taken up and put out of the trial.

15. *Awards.* All awards made by the judge or judges at a Working Trial shall be in accordance with the agreed scale of points approved by the committee of the Kennel Club.

16. *Notification of Awards.* The secretary of a Working Trial shall send (within seven days of the trial) a notification and marked card to the Kennel Club of the names of the prize winners and those dogs to whom the judges have awarded certificates.

17. *Entry Forms.* Entry Forms must be in accordance with the approved form which must be issued by the secretary of the Working Trial meeting, and all entries must be made thereon and not otherwise, and entirely in ink or indelible pencil; only one person shall enter on one form. All such Entry Forms must be preserved by the committee of a Working Trial meeting for at least twelve months from the last day of the trials.

18. *Refusal of Entries.* The committee of any Meeting may reserve to themselves the right of refusing any entries on reasonable grounds.

19. *Objections to Dogs.* An objection to a dog must be made to the secretary in writing at any time within twenty-one days of the last day of the meeting upon the objector lodging with the secretary the sum of £2, which shall be forfeited if the objection proves frivolous. Should any objection be made which cannot at the time be substantiated or disproved, the dog may be allowed to compete under protest, the secretary retaining his winnings until the objection has been withdrawn or decided upon.

When an objection is lodged the secretary of the society must send to the Kennel Club:

(a) A copy of the objection.

(b) The name and address of the objector.

(c) The name and address of the owner of the dog.

(d) All relevant evidence.

The objection will then be dealt with by the committee of the Kennel Club at a meeting of which all persons concerned will receive due notice. The decision of the committee of the Kennel Club shall be final.

No objection shall be invalidated solely on the ground that any notice has not been duly given or that any meeting has not been held under this Regulation.

If the dog objected to be disqualified, the prize to which he would otherwise have been entitled shall be forfeited, and the dog or dogs next in order of merit shall move up and take the prize or prizes.

No spectator, not being the owner of a dog competing, or his accredited representative, has the right to lodge any objection to a dog or to any action taken at the meeting, unless he be a member of the appointed committee, or of the committee of the Kennel Club or a steward. Any objection so lodged will be disregarded.

20. *Withdrawal of Dogs from Competition.* No dog entered for competition, and actually at the meeting, may be withdrawn from competition without the written consent of the stewards.

No competitor may leave the field without the permission of the judges or stewards. Anyone doing so without such permission is liable to disqualification.

BLOODHOUNDS

1. *Entries.* Hounds must be named at the time of making entries, and particulars given in accordance with Rule 1 of the Kennel Club Rules for Working Trials and Obedience Tests.

2. *Order of Running.* At a date prior to the meeting, previously announced, a draw shall take place to determine the order in which hounds shall be run. By mutual agreement owners may vary the order of running, subject to the approval of the stewards.

3. *Qualifying Rounds.* In the case of a large number of entries being received, a Committee may arrange for preliminary qualifying rounds to be worked off at dates prior to the actual meeting, when the hounds winning in the earlier rounds will be brought together.

G

4. *Disqualification for Absence.* The Committee shall announce the hour for beginning each day, and each hound must be brought up in its proper turn without delay. If absent for more than half an hour when called, a hound shall be liable to be disqualified by the judge or judges.

5. *Method of Working.* The Committee may arrange for hounds to be run singly or together in any numbers, provided the conditions are duly announced in the schedule. Hounds must be hunted by owners or their deputies. All hounds entered in any one stake shall be tried in the same way.

6. *Hounds may be required to Wear Collars.* Hounds when hunted together shall wear distinguishing collars if ordered by the judge or judges.

7. *Challenge Certificates.* No hound shall be entitled to win a Kennel Club Working Trial Certificate unless he has clearly identified the runner to the satisfaction of the judge or judges.

THE AMERICAN REGULATIONS FOR OBEDIENCE TRIALS

(*By permission of the American Kennel Club*)

Chapter I

SPECIAL REGULATIONS AND AWARDS APPLYING TO DOGS COMPETING IN OBEDIENCE TRIALS

SECTION 1. If a club or association wishes to hold an Obedience Trial at which points towards a title may be awarded, it must make application to the American Kennel Club for leave to hold such trial. *Such a trial may be held either in connection with a dog show or as a separate event (if an all breed trial is held apart from a dog show it can be given only by an obedience club), but in either case all of the rules applying to dog shows, where applicable, shall govern the conducting of obedience trials and shall apply to all persons participating in them excepting as the following Regulations and Standards for Obedience Trials may provide otherwise and excepting that castrated dogs and sprayed bitches may be entered in obedience trials.* The application shall contain such information as the American Kennel Club may require, and the club or association shall make a deposit of an amount which shall be determined by the American Kennel Club. Such club will be required to make only one date deposit for the two events. If the club is not a member of the American Kennel Club, it shall also pay a license fee for the privilege of holding such trial, the amount of which shall also be determined by the American Kennel Club. The American Kennel Club will notify the club or association of its approval or disapproval of the application. If the club or association shall fail to hold its trial at the time and place which have been approved, the deposit shall become the property of the American Kennel Club, but the amount of any license fee paid will be returned.

(At present the license fee required to be paid for holding an Obedience Trial under above Section 1, by a club that is not a member of the American Kennel Club, is $25.00. The deposit required from each club is $25.00.)

SECTION 2. *If an obedience trial is held by an obedience club, an obedience trial committee must be appointed by the club, and this committee shall exercise all the authority vested in a bench show committee. If an obedience club holds its obedience trial in conjunction with a dog show, then the obedience trial committee shall have sole jurisdiction only over those dogs entered in the obedience trial; provided, however, that if any dog is entered in both obedience and breed classes, then the obedience trial committee shall have jurisdiction over such dog, its owner, and its handler, only in matters pertaining to the Regulations and Standards for Obedience Trials, and the bench show committee shall have jurisdiction over such dog, its owner and handler, in all other matters.*

When an obedience trial is to be held in connection with a dog show by the club or association which has been granted permission to hold that dog show, the club's bench show committee shall include one person to be designated as "obedience chairman". *At this event the bench show committee of the show-giving club shall have sole jurisdiction over all matters which may properly come before it, regardless of whether the matter has to do with the dog show or with the obedience trial.*

SECTION 3. A club or association which has been granted permission to hold a dog show may also be granted permission to hold in connection with the show any or all of the obedience classes defined in this chapter, except Tracking Tests, if in the opinion of the Board of Directors of the American Kennel Club such club or association is qualified to do so.

SECTION 4. *A club or association may hold an obedience match by obtaining the sanction of the American Kennel Club. Sanctioned obedience matches shall be governed by such regulations as may be determined from time to time by the Board of Directors of the American Kennel Club. No score made at a match shall be considered as "qualifying" or as a "leg" towards a degree.*

SECTION 5A. *In the following sections 5, 6, 10, 11 and 16 (as renumbered) of Chapter I, "any breed"* shall mean only those breeds eligible for registration in the American Kennel Club Stud Book or for entry in the Miscellaneous Class at American Kennel Club shows.

SECTION 5. (Novice Class A). The Obedience Novice Class A shall be for pure-bred dogs of any breed and of either sex which have not won the title of "C.D." (Companion Dog). One dog only may be entered in this class by any one exhibitor and every dog in the class must have a separate handler. Dogs entered in this class must be exhibited by the owner or a member of his immediate family. No licensed handler, no trainer nor any kennel employee shall be allowed to compete as exhibitor or otherwise.

SECTION 6. (Novice Class B). The Obedience Novice Class B shall be for pure-bred dogs of any breed and of either sex which have not won the title of "C.D." (Companion Dog). Dogs in this class may be handled or exhibited by the owner or any other person. Exhibitors may enter more than one dog in this class, but each dog must have a separate handler for the "Sit" and "Down" exercises when judged together. No dog may be entered in both Novice Class A and Novice Class B at any one trial.

SECTION 7. The tests and scores for a perfect performance in the Novice Class shall be:

		Points
1.	Heel on Leash	35
2.	Stand for Examination	30
3.	Heel Free	45
4.	Recall	30
5.	Long Sit	30
6.	Long Down	30
	Maximum Total Score	200

(Less Penalty for Misbehaviour)

SECTION 8. The American Kennel Club will permit the use of the letters "C.D.", signifying "Companion Dog", to be used in connection with and after the name of each dog which shall be certified by Judges of Obedience Trials to have received scores of more than 50 per cent of the available points in each of the six exercises and total scores of 170 or more points in Obedience Novice Classes.

SECTION 9. The total number of dogs required to compete in the Novice Class A and Novice Class B combined and the number of Obedience Novice Classes in which a dog must receive a score of more than 50 per cent of the available points in each of the six exercises and a total score of 170 or more points in order to be permitted to use the letters "C.D." shall be fixed and determined by the Board of Directors of the American Kennel Club.

At present, to be permitted to use the letters "C.D.", a dog must receive a score of more than 50 per cent of the available points in each of the six exercises and a total score of 170 or more points in Novice Classes at three Obedience Trials in which the combined number competing in Novice Class A and Novice Class B at each trial shall be six or more dogs. This applies to Division No. 1 (East and North); Division No. 2 (West and South); Division No. 3 (California); Division No. 4 (Pacific Northwest); and Division No. 5 (Hawaii).

SECTION 10. (Open Class A). The Obedience Open Class A shall be for pure-bred dogs of any breed and of either sex which shall have won the title of "C.D." (Companion Dog) in Obedience Novice Classes. One dog only may be entered in this class by any one exhibitor and every dog in the class must have a separate handler who is to handle his dog in all exercises including the "Sit" and the "Down"; dogs entered in this class must be exhibited by the owner or a member of his immediate family. No licensed handler, no trainer nor any kennel employee shall be allowed to compete as exhibitor or otherwise. No dog that has won the title of "C.D.X." shall be entered in this class.

SECTION 11. (Open Class B). The Obedience Open Class B shall be for pure-bred dogs of any breed and of either sex which shall have won the title of "C.D." (Companion Dog). Dogs in this class may be handled or exhibited by the owner or any other person. Exhibitors may enter more than one dog in this class, but the same handler who handled each dog in the first five exercises must handle each dog in the "Sit" and "Down" exercises, except that where a handler has handled more than one dog in the first five exercises, he must have an additional handler for each additional dog when judged together. No dog may be entered in both Open Class A and Open Class B at any one trial.

SECTION 12. The tests and scores for a perfect performance in the Open Classes shall be:

	Points
1. Heel Free	40
2. Drop on Recall	30
3. Retrieve on Flat	25
4. Retrieve over High Jump	35
5. Broad Jump	20
6. Long Sit	25
7. Long Down	25
Maximum Total Score	200

(Less Penalty for Misbehaviour)

SECTION 13. The American Kennel Club will permit the use of the letters "C.D.X.' signifying "Companion Dog Excellent", to be used in connection with and after the name of each dog which shall be certified by Judges of Obedience Trials to have received scores of more than 50 per cent of the available points in each of the seven exercises and total scores of 170 or more points in Obedience Open Classes.

SECTION 14. The total number of dogs required to compete in the Open Class A and Open Class B combined and the number of Obedience Open Classes in which a dog must receive a score of more than 50 per cent of the available points in each of the seven exercises and a total score of 170 or more points in order to be permitted to use the letters "C.D.X." shall be fixed and determined by the Board of Directors of the American Kennel Club.

At present, to be permitted to use the letters "C.D.X.", a dog must receive a score of more than 50 per cent of the available points in each of the seven exercises and a total score of 170 or more points in Open Classes at three Obedience Trials in which the combined number competing in Open Class A and Open Class B at each trial shall be six or more dogs in Division No. 1 (East and North) and Division No. 3 (California), four or more dogs in Division No. 2 (West and South) and Division No. 4 (Pacific Northwest) and three or more dogs in Division No. 5 (Hawaii).

SECTION 15. A dog may continue to compete in the Obedience Open Class B after having won the title of "C.D.X." and/or "U.D.", and may continue to compete in the Utility Class after having won the title of "U.D."

SECTION 16. (Utility Class). The Obedience Utility Class shall be for pure-bred dogs of any breed and of either sex which shall have won the title of "C.D.X." (Companion Dog Excellent) in Obedience Open Classes. Handlers, trainers and kennel employees may compete in this class. Exhibitors may enter more than one dog in this class, but each dog must have a separate handler for the "Group Examination" exercise when judged together.

SECTION 17. The tests and scores for a perfect performance in the Utility Classes shall be:

	Points
1. Scent Discrimination—Article 1	20
2. Secnt Discrimination—Article 2	20
3. Scent Discrimination—Article 3	20
4. Seek Back	30
5. Signal Exercise	35
6. Directed Jumping	40
7. Group Examination	35
Maximum Total Score	200

(Less Penalty for Misbehaviour)

SECTION 18. The American Kennel Club will permit the use of the letters "U.D.," signifying "Utility Dog", to be used in connection with, and after the name of each dog which shall be certified by Judges of Obedience Trials to have received scores of more than 50 per cent of the available points in each of the seven exercises and total scores of 170 or more points in the Obedience Utility Class.

SECTION 19. (Utility Class). The total number of dogs required to compete in the Utility Class and the number of Obedience Utility Classes in which a dog must receive a score of more than 50 per cent of the available points in each of the seven exercises and a total score of 170 or more points in order to be permitted to use the letters "U.D." shall be fixed and determined by the Board of Directors of the American Kennel Club.

At present, to be permitted to use the letters "U.D.", a dog must receive a score of more than 50 per cent of the available points in each of the seven exercises and a total score of 170 or more points in the Utility Class at three Obedience Trials in each of which classes three or more dogs were competing. This applies to Division No. 1 (East and North), Division No. 2 (West and South), Division No. 3 (California), Division No. 4 (Pacific Northwest) and Division No. 5 (Hawaii).

SECTION 20. (Tracking Test). This test must be judged by two judges and is open only to pure-bred dogs. With each entry form of a dog which has not passed a "Tracking Test", there must be filed a written statement by a person who is accredited by the American Kennel Club to judge a "Tracking Test", that the dog is considered by him to be ready for such a test. Handlers, trainers and kennel employees may compete. An exhibitor may enter more than one dog. The holding of other titles, including "T.D.", shall not bar a dog from competition in this test.

This test cannot be given indoors nor at a dog show. The duration of this test may be one day or more, within a fifteen day period from the original date, in the event of an unusually large entry, or other unforeseen emergency, provided that the change in date is satisfactory to the exhibitors affected.

SECTION 21. The American Kennel Club will permit the use of the letters "T.D.", signifying "Tracking Dog" to be used in connection with, and after the name of each dog which shall be certified by the two Judges to have passed a Tracking Test at which at least three dogs have competed.

In case of dogs holding both the "Utility Dog" and "Tracking Dog" titles, these titles may be combined, as "U.D.T." signifying "Utility Dog Tracker".

SECTION 22. The following colours shall be used for prize ribbons in all classes except at sanctioned obedience *matches*:

First Prize	Blue
Second Prize	Red
Third Prize	Yellow
Fourth Prize	White

All prize ribbons shall have the words "Obedience Trial" printed on them.

SECTION 23. If ribbons are given at sanctioned obedience *matches*, they shall be of the following colours:

First Prize	Rose
Second Prize	Brown
Third Prize	Light Green
Fourth Prize	Grey

All prize ribbons shall have the words "Obedience Trial" printed on them.

SECTION 24. Bitches in season are not permitted to compete. The Judge of an Obedience Trial or Tracking Test must remove from competition any bitch in season, any dog which does not obey its handler, any handler who interferes wilfully with another competitor, or his dog, and may expel from competition any dog which he considers unfit to compete, or any bitch which appears so attractive to males as to be a disturbing element. In case of doubt an official veterinarian shall be called to give his opinion.

SECTION 25. The owner or agent entering a dog in an Obedience Trial does so at his own risk and agrees to abide by the rules of the American Kennel Club, and the regulations and Standards for Obedience Trials.

SECTION 26. The decisions of the Obedience Trial Committee or the Bench Show Committee, if the trial be held by a show-giving club, shall be conclusive in all matters arising at the trial and shall bind all parties, subject however, to the rules of the American Kennel Club.

SECTION 27. Any dog entered and received at an Obedience Trial must compete in all exercises of all classes in which it is entered, unless expelled by the Judge or excused by the official veterinarian. *The excuse by the official veterinarian must be in writing and attached to the show or trial report sent to the American Kennel Club by the superintendant, show secretary or trial secretary. If a dog is expelled by a judge, the reason shall be stated in the Judge's book.*

SECTION 28.   No dog belonging wholly or in part to any Judge, or to any member of the immediate family or household of any Judge, shall be entered or exhibited in any dog show, Obedience Trial or Tracking Test at which such person may judge. This applies to both obedience and dog show Judges when an Obedience Trial is held in conjunction with a dog show. However, a Tracking Test held on a different day shall be considered a separate event for the purpose of this section.

SECTION 29.   No entry shall be made at any Obedience Trial or Tracking Test under a judge of any dog which the Judge, or any member of his immediate family, or household, has owned, sold, held under lease, handled in the ring, boarded, trained, or instructed regularly, within one year prior to the date of the trial. This includes Judges who train professionally, or as amateurs, and applies equally to judges who train individual dogs, and those who train dogs in classes with or through their handlers. However, the above limitations as to trainers shall not apply at sanctioned matches.

SECTION 30.   In order to win a "C.D.", "C.D.X.", or "U.D." degree, qualifying scores must be obtained under at least three different Judges.

SECTION 31.   At outdoor tests held at dog shows a separate ring (rings) shall be provided for obedience classes and a sign forbidding any dog to enter such rings, except when being judged, shall be erected by the Superintendent and it shall be his duty as well as that of the Obedience Trial (or Bench Show) Committee to enforce this regulation. At indoor tests where limited space does not permit the exclusive use of rings for obedience tests, the same regulations will apply after the obedience rings have been set up.

SECTION 32.   Where any of the foregoing sections of the Regulations excludes from a particular Obedience Class dogs which have won a particular Obedience title, eligibility to enter that class shall be determined as follows: A dog may continue to be exhibited in such a class after his handler has been notified by three different Judges that he has received three qualiyfing scores for such title, but may not be entered or exhibited in such a class in any Obedience Trial of which the closing date for entries occurs after the owner has received official notification from the American Kennel Club that the dog has won the particular Obedience title.

SECTION 33.   Where any of the foregoing sections of the Regulations requires that a dog shall have won a particular Obedience title before being entered in a particular Obedience class, a dog may not be entered or exhibited in such class at any Obedience Trial for which entries have closed before the owner has received official notification from the American Kennel Club that the dog has won the required title.

SECTION 34.   *Prizes and trophies at an Obedience Trial must be offered to be won outright and to be awarded automatically on the basis of scores attained by dogs competing at the Trial with the exception that a trophy or prize which requires three wins by the same exhibitor, not necessarily with the same dog, for permanent possession, may be offered for the highest scoring dog in the trial or the highest scoring dog in one of the classes.*

Class prize ribbons and trophies offered for the four official placings in a class shall be awarded on the basis of total final scores without regard to more than 50 per cent of the points required for a qualifying score in each exercise.

Such other trophies and prizes as are offered for outright and automatic award in any class, or in any section of a split class, including prizes or trophies for the highest scoring dog in the trial or for the dog with the highest combined score in the Open "B" and Utility Classes, may stipulate a condition that the score or scores be "qualifying".

SECTION 35.   A club or association holding an Obedience Trial (either a separate event or in combination with a dog show) must prepare, after the entries have closed and not before, a programme showing the time scheduled for the judging of the various classes.

This programme shall be based on the judging of eight Novice entries, seven Open entries or six Utility entries per hour which will be considered a reasonable average and no judge should be called upon to exceed those averages during the period of the advertised hours of a show's and/or trial's duration, less reasonable intermissions for meals. The advertised hours of a show's and/or trial's duration shall be considered the time from the start of judging to the closing of the show.

Each judge's assignment must be scheduled so as to insure the completion of the judging (based on the formula above) prior to the closing hour of the show and/or trial.

If indications point to a probable entry in any or all classes in excess of a club's facilities, it may limit entries in any or all classes by prominent announcement on the title or cover page of its premium list (or immediately under the obedience heading in the premium list of a combined dog show and Obedience Trial) that entries in such class, classes or trial, automatically will close when a certain limit, determined as above, for such class, classes or trial has been received, even if the official closing date for entries has not arrived.

If a club chooses not to so limit its entries and if, upon the closing of entries, it is determined that the entries of any Judge exceed the above hourly averages by more than 15 per cent, then the club shall immediately obtain the approval of the American Kennel Club (a) for a reassignment of its advertised Judges so that the duties of no Judge shall exceed the above schedule by more than 15 per cent or (b) for the appointment of an additional Judge to share the class assignment with the advertised Judge whose entries are excessive. In the latter case, immediately after obtaining approval of such additional Judge, the Obedience Trial (or bench show) committee shall, by the drawing of lots, divide the entry between the two Judges. Immediately after obtaining approval of either such change, the club shall mail to the exhibitor of each entry so affected, a notification of the change of Judge and the exhibitor shall be permitted to withdraw such entries at any time prior to the opening day of the show and the entry fees paid for entering such dogs shall be refunded. The club, in such notice to exhibitors, shall also announce which of the two Judges of a given class will judge the run-off of any tie scores which may finally develop as between the two groups of dogs. Each Judge, however, shall first conduct the run-off of any ties developing in his own group of dogs.

A club may choose to announce two Judges for a given class in its premium list. In such case the entries shall be divided by lot as above provided, but no announcement of such drawing need be made to exhibitors in advance of the trial and no exhibitor shall be entitled to a refund of entry fee.

One of the Judges so announced shall be designated in the Premium List as the Judge for the run-off of any tie scores which may finally develop as between the two groups of dogs or if the club desires, and so indicates in its Premium List, a third Judge may be announced for the run-off of such ties.

A club which gives a split class shall not award American Kennel Club official ribbons in either section, but may offer prizes and trophies on the basis of scores made within each section. The four dogs with the highest scores in the class (regardless of the section in which they were made) shall be called back into the ring and awarded the four American Kennel Club official ribbons, by at least one of the Judges of the class, who shall be responsible for recording the entry numbers of the four placed dogs in one of the Judges' Books.

Chapter II

STANDARD FOR OBEDIENCE TRIALS

SECTION 1. The purpose of Obedience Trials is to demonstrate the usefulness of the pure-bred dog as the companion and guardian of man, and not the ability of the dog to acquire facility in the performance of mere tricks. The classification which has been adopted is progressive, with the thought in mind that a dog which can be termed a utility dog has demonstrated his fitness to a place in our modern scheme of living.

SECTION 2. *If the exercises take place indoors, the ring should be at least 30 ft. wide and 50 ft. long and shall under no circumstances be less than 30 ft. wide and 40 ft. long. The ring must be thoroughly cleaned immediately before the judging starts if it has previously been used for breed judging.* The floor shall have a surface or covering adequate to provide firm footing for the largest dogs and rubber or similar non-slip material for the take-off and landing at all jumps. If the exercises take place out-of-doors the ring shall be at least 40 ft. wide and 70 ft. long. The ground shall be level and the grass, if any, shall be cut short.

If inclement weather at an outdoor event makes necessary the judging of Obedience Classes under shelter, all requirements as to ring size shall be waived.

SECTION 3. A word of praise is allowed between exercises and between separate parts of individual exercises after the Judge has said "Exercise finished", but no offering of any kind of food may be given in the ring. All exercises, except "Heel on Leash", "Stand for Examination" and "Tracking", shall be performed off leash.

In the Novice and Open Classes the dog may be put on leash or guided gently by the collar between exercises and to get it into proper position for the next exercise. In the

Utility Class the dog shall not be put on the leash or guided or controlled by the collar at any time, and the leash shall be left on the Judge's table from the time the dog enters the ring until it leaves.

Inperfections in heeling between exercises will not be judged, but any disciplining by the handler in the ring, or any uncontrolled behaviour of the dog, such as snapping, unjustified barking, or running out of the ring, even between exercises, will be severely penalized by deducting points from the total score, and the Judge may bar the dog from further competition at that trial.

SECTION 4.   In all parts of all exercises performed in the ring, a single command or signal only may be given by the handler, and any extra commands or signals, or the giving of a command and a signal must be penalized; except that wherever the standard specifies "command and/or signal" the handler may give either one or the other, or both "command" and "signal" simultaneously. Where a signal is permitted and given, it must be a single gesture with *one* arm and hand only and the arm must be promptly returned to its normal position, *except that both arms may be used simultaneously to call the dog in the Recall Exercises.* Signals must be inaudible and the handler shall not touch the dog. Signalling correction to the dog from a distance is forbidden and must be penalized. Any unusual noises or motions may be considered to be signals. The dog's name may be used once immediately before any verbal command *but may not be used when a signal is employed even though the standard specifies "command and/or signal".* Whistling or the use of a whistle is prohibited.

SECTION 5.   HEEL ON LEASH: In the Novice classes the handler shall enter the ring with his dog on a loose leash and shall stand still with dog sitting at heel at the handler's left side until the Judge asks if the handler is ready and then gives the order "Forward", at which order the handler may attract his dog's attention by saying his name and will give the command to Heel, and at the same time start walking briskly with the dog on loose leash. At the command or signal to Heel the dog shall walk close to the left side of the handler without crowding, permitting the handler freedom of motion at all times. At each order to "Halt", the handler will stop and his dog shall sit smartly at heel without command or signal and not move until ordered to do so. It is permissible after each halt before moving again for the handler to give the command or signal to Heel. Any tightening or jerking of the leash or any act, signal or command which in the opinion of the Judge gives the dog unnecessary or unfair assistance shall be penalized. The judge will give the orders, "Forward", "Halt", "Right turn", "Left turn", "About turn", "Slow", "Normal" and "Fast", which last order signifies that the handler and dog must run. These orders may be given in any sequence and may be repeated if necessary. In executing the "About turn" the handler will do a "Right about turn" in all cases. The Judge will order the handler to execute the "Figure eight" which signifies that the handler shall walk around and between the two stewards who shall stand about 8 ft apart, or if there is only one steward, shall walk around and between the Judge and the steward. The "Figure eight" in the Novice Classes shall be done on leash only. The Judge will say "exercise finished" after the heeling and then, "Are you ready?" before starting the "Figure eight". There shall be no "About turn" in the "Figure eight", but the handler and dog shall go twice completely around the "Figure eight" with at least one halt during and another halt at the end of the exercises.

SECTION 6.   STAND FOR EXAMINATION: The Judge will give the order for examination and the handler will stand or pose his dog, give the command and/or signal to "Stay", walk in front of his dog, turn around, and stand facing his dog at the end of a loose leash. The Judge will touch the dog's head, body and hind quarters only and then give the order, "Back to your dog", whereupon the handler will walk around behind his dog to the heel position. The dog must remain in a standing position until the Judge says, "Exercise finished". The dog must show no shyness nor resentment.

SECTION 7.   HEEL FREE: This shall be executed in the same manner as "Heel on Leash" except that the dog is off the leash. The leash shall be left on the Judge's table for all work done in the "Heel Free" exercise. Heeling in both Novice and Open Classes is done in the same manner except that in the Open Classes the dog does not heel on leash but all work is done off leash, including the "Figure eight".

SECTION 8.   RECALL: To execute the "Recall" to handler, upon order or signal from the Judge, "Leave your dog", the dog is given the command and/or signal to stay in the sitting position while the handler moves *towards* the other end of the ring, the distance to be about 40 ft. Upon order or signal from the Judge, "Call your dog", the handler calls or signals the dog, which in the Novice Class must come straight in at a smart pace and sit immediately in front of the handler. Upon order or signal from the Judge to "Finish", the dog on command or signal must go smartly to heel. In the Open Class, at a point designated by the Judge, the dog must drop on command or signal from the handler, and then on order or signal from the Judge, the handler calls or signals the dog which must rise and come straight in at a smart pace and sit immediately in front of the handler. Upon order or signal from the Judge to "Finish", the dog on command or signal must go smartly to heel.

SECTION 9. LONG SIT: In the "Long Sit" in the Novice Classes all the competing dogs in a class take this exercise together, except that if there are more than fifteen dogs, they shall be split into groups of not less than six nor more than fifteen dogs. Where the same Judge does both classes the separate classes may be combined. The dogs which are in the ring shall be lined up in catalogue order. Handlers' armbands, weighted with leashes, or other articles, if necessary, shall be placed behind the dogs. On order from the Judge the handlers shall sit their dogs and on further order from the Judge to "Leave your dogs" the handlers shall give the command and/or signal to stay and immediately leave their dogs, go to the opposite side of the ring, and line up in front of their respective dogs. In the Novice Classes the Judge shall take a position in the ring where he can observe both the dogs and the handlers. After one minute from the time he has ordered the handlers to leave their dogs, the Judge will order the handlers "Back to your dogs", whereupon the handlers must return promptly to their dogs, each walking around and in back of his own dog to the heel position. The dogs must not move from the sitting position until permission has been given by their respective handlers after the Judge says "Exercise finished".

SECTION 10. LONG DOWN: The "Long Down" in the Novice Classes is done in the same manner as the "Long Sit" except that instead of sitting the dogs the handlers, on orders from the Judge, will down their dogs, and except further, that the time is three minutes. The dog must stay in the down position until after the Judge says, "Exercise finished". The dogs are not required to sit.

SECTION 11. The "Long Sit" and "Long Down" exercises in the Open Classes are performed in the same manner as in the Novice Classes except that after leaving their dogs the handlers must immediately leave the ring and go to a place designated by the Judge out of sight of their dogs, where they must remain until the time limit of three minutes in the "Long Sit" and five minutes in the "Long Down" (from the time the Judge gave the order to "Leave your dogs") has expired.

SECTION 12. RETRIEVE ON FLAT: In "retrieving the Dumb-bell on the Flat", the orders given by the Judge shall be "Throw it", whereupon the handler may give the command and/or signal to stay and throws the dumb-bell: "Send him", whereupon the handler gives a command or signal to his dog to retrieve; "Take it", whereupon the handler may give a command or signal and takes the dumb-bell from the dog; "Finish", whereupon the handler gives the command or signal to heel. The dog shall not move forward to retrieve nor deliver to hand on return until ordered by the handler. The retrieve shall be executed at a fast trot or gallop, without unnecessary mouthing or playing with the dumb-bell. After delivering the dumb-bell from in front of the handler, the dog upon command or signal from the handler shall go to heel position. The size of the dumb-bell may vary with the size of the dog.

SECTION 13. RETRIEVE OVER HIGH JUMP: In "Retrieving the Dumb-bell over the High Jump", the exercise is executed in the same manner as the "Retrieve on the Flat", except that the dog must jump the obstacle both going and coming. The high jump shall be jumped clear and the jump shall be as near as possible one and one-half times the height of the dog at the withers or 3 ft., whichever is less. This applies to all breeds except those listed below for which the jump shall be once the height of the dog at the withers or 3 ft., whichever is less: Bull-mastiffs, Great Danes, Great Pyrenees, Mastiffs, Newfoundlands and St. Bernards.

The side posts of the "High Jump" shall be 4 ft. high and the jump shall be 5 feet wide and shall be so constructed as to provide adjustment for each 2 in. from 12 in. to 36 in. It is suggested that the jump have a bottom board 8 in. wide including the space from the bottom of the board to the ground, together with three other 8-in. boards, one 6-in. board, and one 4-in. board. The jump shall be painted a flat white. The width in inches shall be painted on each side of each board in black 2-in. figures, the figure on the bottom board representing the distance from the ground to the top of the board.

SECTION 14. BROAD JUMP: In the "Broad Jump", the handler will stand with his dog at the heel position in front of and within 10 ft. of the jump. On order from the Judge to "Leave your dog", the handler will give his dog the command and/or signal to stay and go to a position facing the right side of the jump, about 2 ft. from the jump, and within the range of the first and last hurdles. On order from the Judge, the handler shall give the command or signal to jump and the dog shall clear the entire width of the broad jump without touching and, without further command or signal, return to a sitting position immediately in front of the handler as in the "Recall". The handler shall change his position while the dog is in mid-air by executing a right face. On order from the Judge, the handler will give the command or signal to heel and the dog shall finish in the prescribed manner. The Broad Jump shall consist of four separate hurdles, built to telescope for convenience, the largest measuring about 5 ft. wide and 7 in. high at the highest point and painted a flat white. When set up, they shall be spaced so as to cover a distance equal to twice the height of the high jump as set for the particular dog. Hurdles shall be removed in proportion to the height of the dog and the highest hurdles shall be removed first.

SECTION 15. SCENT DISCRIMINATION: In each of these three exercises, the dog must select by scent alone and retrieve an article which has been handled by his handler. The articles shall be provided by the handler and these shall consist of three sets, each comprised by five identical articles, one set being wood, one metal and one leather. The articles in a set must be legibly numbered one to five. The handler shall present all the articles to the Judge and the Judge shall designate one article from each of the three sets. These handlers' articles shall be kept on the Judge's table until picked up by the handler who shall hold in his hand only one article at a time. Immediately after picking up an article, and before imparting the scent, the handler must show the number on the article to the Judge and one of the stewards. The handler's scent may be imparted to the article only from his hands which must remain in plain sight. The handler may pick up his articles in any order. At the start of the "Scent Discrimination" exercises, the remaining twelve articles will be placed at random in the ring about 6 in. apart. The handler will stand about 15 ft. from the articles with the dog sitting at heel position with its back to the articles, and on order from the Judge, the handler immediately will place his article on the Judge's book and the Judge will place it among the other articles. On order from the Judge to "Send him", the handler and the dog will turn to face the articles, and the handler may place his hand gently over the dog's nose and shall give the command or signal to get it. The dog shall go at a brisk pace to the articles, but may take any reasonable time to select the right article provided he works continuously and does not pick up any article other than his handler's. After picking up the right article the dog shall bring it smartly to his handler, and the exercise is completed as in the retrieve exercises. The same procedure is followed in each of the three "Scent Discrimination" exercises. Should a dog retrieve a wrong article in any of the three exercises, it shall be placed on the Judge's table, and the handler's article must also be taken up from the remaining articles. The remaining exercises shall then be completed with fewer than twelve articles left in the ring. At the close of these exercises, the articles shall be removed from the ring.

SECTION 16. SEEK BACK: In the "Seek Back" the handler will stand with his dog in the heel position and, on order from the Judge, will signal or command his dog to walk at heel, and then on specific order or signal from the Judge will execute such portions of the "Heel Free" exercise as the Judge may order. On order from the Judge to drop it, the handler will surreptitiously drop an article as he is walking with his dog at heel. The article must be approved by the Judge and must not be a conspicuous one nor white in colour. After the handler and dog have proceeded about 30 ft. following the dropping of the article, on order or signal from the Judge, the handler will halt with his dog. Then on order or signal from the Judge the handler gives the command to seek back and retrieve the article. The handler should not point to the object but may point in the direction of the trail, and he is to remain in the place from which the dog is sent. The dog may retrieve either by sight or scent and is expected to find the article, pick it up, promptly return to the handler and sit in front of him, holding the article. On command or signal from the Judge, the handler takes the article and may signal or command the dog to give it up. After delivering the article from in front of the handler, the dog, upon command or signal from the handler, shall go to heel position.

SECTION 17. SIGNAL EXERCISE: In the "Signal Exercise" the heeling is done in the same manner as in the "Heel Free" exercise except that throughout the entire exercise the handler uses signals only and must not speak to his dog at any time. On order or signal from the Judge "Forward", the handler signals his dog to walk at heel and then, on specific order or signal from the Judge in each case, the handler and dog execute a "Left turn", "Right turn", "About turn", "Halt", "Slow", "Normal", "Fast". These orders may be given in any sequence and may be repeated if necessary. Then, on order or signal from the Judge, the handler signals his dog to "stand" in the heel position near the end of the ring, and on further order or signal from the Judge "Leave your dog", the handler signals his dog to stay, goes to the far end of the ring, and turns to face his dog. Then, on separate and specific signals from the Judge in each case, the handler will give the signals to drop, to sit, to come to a sit in front, and to finish, after which the Judge will say "Exercise finished". During the heeling part of this exercise the handler may not give any signal except where a command or signal is permitted in the Heeling Exercises.

SECTION 18. DIRECTED JUMPING: In the "Directed Jumping" exercise the jumps shall be placed midway the ring and as close to the sides *as is practicable and between* 20 *and* 30 *ft. apart.* (The Bar Jump on one side, the Hurdle on the other.) The handler from a position on the centre line of the ring and about 20 ft. from *the line of* the jumps, stands with his dog in the heel position. On order or signal, "Send him" from the Judge, he commands and/or signals his dog to go forward at a smart pace to the other end of the ring to an equal distance beyond the jumps and in the approximate centre where the handler stops his dog by command, whereupon the dog must stop and sit, with his attention on the handler (the dog need not sit squarely at this point). The Judge will then designate which jump is to be taken first by the dog, whereupon the handler commands and/or signals his dog *to return to him over the designated jump, the dog sitting in front of the handler and finishing as in the "Recall".* The handler may also give a command *to jump at each jump, but the word used must be different from the word used to call the dog.* A signal used in either case, must be a single gesture with the arm and hand only, and the arm must be promptly returned to its normal position. While the dog is in mid-air the handler may turn to right or left so as to be facing the dog when it lands from the jump. *The Judge will say "Exercise finished" after the dog has returned to the heel position, at which time a word of praise is permitted. When the dog is again in heel position for the second part of the exercise, the Judge will ask "Are you ready?" before giving the order or signal "Send him" for the second jump.* The same procedure is to be followed for the dog taking the opposite jump. It is optional with the Judge which jump is taken first but both jumps must be taken to complete the exercise and the Judge must not designate the jump until the dog is at the far end of the ring. The height of the jumps shall be the same as required in the Open Classes. The high jump shall be the same as that used in the Open Classes, and the bar jump shall consist of a bar between 2 and 2½ in. in diameter, painted black and white in alternate sections of about 3 in. each. The bar shall be supported by two 4-ft. upright posts at least 5 ft. apart. The bar shall be adjustable for each 2 in. of height from 12 in. to 36 in. and shall be so constructed that the bar can be knocked off without disturbing the uprights. The dog shall clear the jumps without touching them.

SECTION 19. GROUP EXAMINATION: All the competing dogs take this exercise together, except that if there are more than fifteen dogs, they shall be split into groups of not less than six nor more than fifteen dogs. The handlers and dogs which are in the ring shall line up in catalogue order, side by side down the centre of the ring with the dogs at heel position. Each handler shall place his armband, weighted if necessary, behind his dog. On order from the Judge to "Stand your dogs", all the handlers will stand or pose their dogs, and on order from the Judge, "Leave your dogs", all the handlers will give the command and/or signal to "Stay" and walk forward to the side of the ring, then about turn and face their dogs. The Judge will approach each dog in turn from the front and examine each dog as in conformation judging. After all dogs have been examined, and after the handlers have been away from their dogs for at least three minutes, the Judge will order the handlers, "Back to your dogs", and the handlers will walk around behind their dogs to the heel position, after which the Judge will say, "Exercise finished". Each dog must remain standing at his position in the line, from the time his handler leaves him until the end of the exercise, and must show no shyness nor resentment.

SECTION 20. TRACKING: The tracking test must be performed with the dog on leash, the length of the track to be not less than 440 yards nor more than 500 yards, the scent to be not less than one half hour nor more than two hours old and that of a stranger who will leave a leather glove or wallet to be found at the end of the track. The tracklayer will follow the track (which has been staked out with flags a day or more earlier) collecting all the flags on the way with exception of one flag at the start of the track and one flag not more than 30 yds. from the start of the track to indicate the direction of the track; then deposit the article at the end of the track, and leave the course, proceeding straight ahead at least 50 ft. The tracklayers must wear leather-soled shoes. The length of the leash used in tracking must be 30 to 60 ft. and the dog must work at this length with no help from the handler. A dog may, at the handler's option, be given one, and only one, second chance to take the scent between the two flags at the start, provided he has not passed the second flag.

The Standards for Judging and Judging Charts can be obtained from The American Kennel Club, 221 Fourth Avenue, New York 3, N.Y.

CPSIA information can be obtained at www.ICGtesting.com
Printed in the USA
LVOW11s2127080215

426214LV00001B/36/P